SOCIALISM

· A · GARLAND · FOR · MAY · DAY · 1895 ·
· DEDICATED · TO · THE · WORKERS · BY · WALTER · CRANE ·

SOCIALISM

·

Michael Newman

A BRIEF
INSIGHT

STERLING

New York / London
www.sterlingpublishing.com

STERLING and the distinctive Sterling logo are registered trademarks of
Sterling Publishing Co., Inc.

Library of Congress Cataloging-in-Publication Data available

10 9 8 7 6 5 4 3 2 1

Published by Sterling Publishing Co., Inc.
387 Park Avenue South, New York, NY 10016

Published by arrangement with Oxford University Press, Inc.

© 2005 by Michael Newman
Illustrated edition published in 2010 by Sterling Publishing Co., Inc.
Additional text © 2010 Sterling Publishing Co., Inc.

Distributed in Canada by Sterling Publishing
c/o Canadian Manda Group, 165 Dufferin Street
Toronto, Ontario, Canada M6K 3H6

Book design: Faceout Studio

Please see picture credits on page 207 for image copyright information.

Printed in China
All rights reserved

Sterling ISBN 978-1-4027-7537-6

For information about custom editions, special sales, premium and corporate purchases, please contact
Sterling Special Sales Department at 800-805-5489 or specialsales@sterlingpublishing.com.

Frontispiece: The English artist Walter Crane (1845–1915) was not only a prominent illustrator of
children's books, he was a committed socialist as well. This illustration was published in the magazine
Clarion in 1895 to commemorate May Day, the international workers' holiday.

CONTENTS

•

ACKNOWLEDGMENTS

•

Writing a very short book on a vast subject has been a great challenge, and I am grateful to all those at Oxford University Press who have given me this opportunity. In particular, I would like to thank Marsha Filion for her helpful suggestions and Alyson Lacewing for her skilful copyediting. I very much appreciate the comments on earlier drafts by Kate Soper, Richard Kuper, Marjorie Mayo, my daughter Kate, and an anonymous referee. I am also conscious of many people who have influenced my thinking about socialism, particularly the late Peter Seltman, an inspiring colleague to whose memory I would like to dedicate this work. But as always, I owe most of all to Ines for her constant encouragement and support, our ongoing dialogue on the subject matter, and her cogent criticisms.

My aims have been to provide an accessible introduction while simultaneously providing food for thought on a controversial topic. I hope not to cause those who disagree with my interpretation too much indigestion!

INTRODUCTION

•

IN 1867 KARL MARX ended the first volume of his monumental work *Das Kapital* on a triumphant note. A point would be reached, he argued, when the capitalist system would "burst asunder" and at this stage:

> The knell of capitalist private property sounds. The expropriators are expropriated.

For more than a hundred years many socialists believed, and many of their opponents feared, that Marx had been right: capitalism was doomed and would be replaced by socialism. How things have changed! In recent years, and particularly since the collapse of the Soviet bloc between 1989 and 1991, a dramatic reversal has taken place. It is now capitalism that is triumphant, and many regard socialism as an historical relic which will probably die out during the course of the current century. I do not share this belief, and the final chapter of this book seeks to demonstrate the continuing and contemporary relevance of socialism. But whether or not the reader will agree with this conclusion,

This gathering of socialists took place in New York City's Union Square on May 1, 1912.

I hope that the book will at least provide clarification and discussion as a basis for judgment.

The first, and crucial, question is: what is socialism? Those who attack or defend socialism often take its meaning as self-evident. Thus the opponents of all forms of socialism have been keen to dismiss the whole idea by equating it with its most repellent manifestations—particularly the Stalinist dictatorship in the Soviet Union from the late 1920s until 1953. Similarly, its proponents have tended to identify socialism with the particular form that they have favored. Lenin therefore once defined it as "soviet power plus electrification," while a British politician, Herbert Morrison, argued that socialism was "what a Labour government does." Yet socialism has taken far too many forms to be constricted in these ways. Indeed, some have viewed it primarily as a set of values and theories and have denied that the policies of any state or political party have had any relevance for the evaluation of socialism as a doctrine. This purist position lies at the other extreme from that of Lenin and Morrison and is equally unhelpful. In fact, socialism has been both centralist and local; organized from above and built from below; visionary and pragmatic; revolutionary and reformist; anti-state and statist; internationalist and nationalist; harnessed to political parties and shunning them; an outgrowth of trade unionism and independent of it; a feature of rich industrialized countries and poor peasant-based communities; sexist and feminist; committed to growth and ecological.

One way of discussing so diverse a phenomenon is to claim that all forms of socialism share some fundamental characteristic, or essence, by which the doctrine as a whole may be defined. Certainly, this would simplify analysis, but this essentialist approach normally degenerates into rather dogmatic assertions about the nature of "true socialism" and becomes a weapon to use against the heretics. However, there are equal dangers in defining socialism so broadly that the subject cannot be analyzed meaningfully. This book seeks to overcome these contradictory dangers by taking the following minimal definitions of socialism as guidelines.

In my view, the most fundamental characteristic of socialism is its commitment to the creation of an egalitarian society. Socialists may not have agreed about the extent to which inequality can be eradicated or the means by which change can be effected, but no socialist would defend the current inequalities of wealth and power. In particular, socialists have maintained that, under capitalism, vast privileges and opportunities are derived from the hereditary ownership of capital and wealth at one end of the social scale, while a cycle of deprivation limits opportunities and influence at the other end. To varying extents, all socialists have therefore challenged the property relationships that are fundamental to capitalism, and have aspired to establish a society in which everyone has the possibility to seek fulfillment without facing barriers based on structural inequalities.

A second, and closely related, common feature of socialism has been a belief in the possibility of constructing an alternative egalitarian system based on the values of solidarity and cooperation. But this in turn has depended on a third characteristic: a relatively optimistic view of human beings and their ability to cooperate with one another. The extent, both of the optimism and its necessity for the construction of a new society, varies considerably. For those who believe in the possibility of establishing self-governing communities without hierarchy or law, the optimistic conception of "human nature" is essential. For others who have favored hierarchical parties and states, such optimism could be more limited. It is also no doubt true that, in the world after Nazism and Stalinism, the optimism of some earlier thinkers has been tempered by harsh realities. Nevertheless, socialists have always rejected views that stress individual self-interest and competition as the sole motivating factors of human behavior in all societies at all times. They have regarded this perspective as the product of a particular kind of society, rather than as an ineradicable fact about human beings.

Finally, most socialists have been convinced that it is possible to make significant changes in the world through conscious human agency. It is true that some interpreters of Marx have stressed economic determinism to such an extent that their belief in the role of people in bringing about change has sometimes been difficult to discern. Nevertheless, in general, passive resignation to the existing situation is alien to socialists. They have shared this view with capitalists and liberals, while opposing them in other respects. For capitalism, liberalism, and socialism are all products of the modern era in their belief that human beings may act as subjects of history, rather than having their fortunes determined by fate, custom, tradition, or religion.

These common characteristics help to distinguish socialism from other doctrines, ideologies, and systems, but it is also very diverse. This is not surprising when its evolution and development are considered. If modern socialism was born in nineteenth-century Europe, it was subsequently shaped by, and adapted to, a whole range of societies. For example, the emergence of communism as a separate strand of socialism following the Revolution in Russia in 1917 (see Chapter 1) strengthened its appeal in many developing countries that were still controlled by European empires. However, communism was also to assume different forms as it was tailored to local conditions and merged with movements for national independence. Long before the Chinese communists assumed control of the country in 1949, it was clear that their new leader, Mao Zedong (1893–1976), had

Subsequent to the Russian Revolution, many Russian farmers voluntarily formed *kolkhozy*—or collective farms—in order to share the responsibilities and resources of agricultural production in the new socialist economy. This photograph of two men building a log house on a *kolkhoz* near Gorky, Russia, was taken some time between 1920 and 1924.

emphasized the continuing role of the peasantry to a much greater extent than his Soviet counterparts, and by the 1960s there were serious clashes between these two communist superpowers. Meanwhile, other communist regimes that had emerged in North Korea and Vietnam were shaped by specific conditions of civil war, struggles for national liberation, and American intervention. Elsewhere quite different forms of socialism emerged. For example, some of the Jewish settlers in Palestine sought to establish small-scale cooperative communities in the so-called Kibbutz movement long before the establishment of Israel in 1948; subsequently many Arab states, beginning with Egypt in the 1950s, turned to a version of secular socialism, modernizing dictatorship and nationalism fueled in part by the existence of Israel and Western domination. In postcolonial Africa, particularly in Ghana in 1957 and Tanzania in the 1960s, quite different attempts were made to marry elements of socialism with local traditions. Similarly, in Latin America various experiments have been tried, but have normally been defeated, particularly because of the overwhelming power and presence of the United States. The most enduring exception, to which particular attention will be paid in Chapter 2, is that of Cuba under Fidel Castro which, since 1959, has combined a national social revolution with elements of the Soviet model.

Ideally, a book on socialism would discuss the whole world, but this is clearly not possible in a very short book. There are also many important issues—perhaps particularly those concerning ethnicity, nationalism, and global inequality—that cannot be addressed adequately here. Instead, I have attempted to examine some aspects of socialism in more depth than would be possible in a general survey, and have also made use of case studies. Chapter 1 looks at the foundations of the doctrine by examining the contribution made by various traditions of socialism in the period between the early nineteenth century and the aftermath of the First World War. The two forms that emerged as dominant by the early 1920s were social democracy and communism, and Chapter 2 analyzes the experience of Sweden in relation to the former and Cuba in relation to the latter. Despite their dominance, both communism and social democracy were increasingly challenged from the 1960s, and Chapter 3 seeks to elucidate this by exploring two further case studies—feminism and the Green movement. These new social movements raised both theoretical and organizational issues that had not previously been addressed—or addressed sufficiently. Traditionalists feared that these movements would fragment socialism, but I will argue here that they also enriched it. The final chapter seeks to explain the pressures on socialism during the last quarter century and to account for its current difficulties. It ends by reconsidering some key ideas in the light of experience and suggests the kind of socialism that will remain relevant in the twenty-first century.

ONE

Socialist Traditions

•

SOME HAVE TRACED THE ORIGINS of socialist doctrine to Plato, others to Christianity, and many, with greater plausibility, to radical movements in the English Civil War in the seventeenth century. However, modern socialism, with its evolving and continuous set of ideas and movements, emerged in early nineteenth-century Europe. The reasons for this have long been debated, but it is widely agreed that very rapid economic and social changes, associated with urbanization and industrialization, were of particular importance. These not only undermined the rural economy, but also led to a breakdown of the norms and values that had underpinned the traditional order. Liberals of the era welcomed

This 1801 oil painting by Philippe-Jacques de Loutherbourg (1740–1812) depicts the Bedlam Furnaces in Coalbrookdale, a valley situated on the river Severn in England's Shropshire county. The Bedlam Furnaces were one of the earliest furnaces to use coke instead of coal to smelt iron. Coalbrookdale is considered one of the birthplaces of the Industrial Revolution; Britain's first iron rails, iron bridge, iron boat, and steam locomotive were produced in this region.

this transformation, regarding capitalist enterprise and the new individualism as the embodiment of progress and freedom. However, socialists dissented from two aspects of the liberals' outlook. First, rather than individualism, they tended to emphasize community, cooperation, and association—qualities that they believed to be jeopardized by contemporary developments. And, second, rather than celebrating the proclaimed progress arising from capitalist enterprise, they were preoccupied by the massive inequality that it was causing, as former peasants and artisans were herded into overcrowded towns and forced to work in new factories for pitifully low wages. It was in this context that the term "socialist" was first used in the *London Co-operative Magazine* in 1827, which suggested that the great issue was whether it was more beneficial that capital should be owned individually or held in common. Those who believed the latter were "the Communionists and Socialists." This chapter will examine some of the distinct traditions that then emerged.

The Utopians

The label "utopian" was subsequently attached to some of the early socialists by Karl Marx and Friedrich Engels. It was intended to convey negative attitudes toward them, suggesting naïveté and a failure to root their ideas in rigorous social, economic, and political analysis. More generally, the notion of "utopianism" has often been used to dismiss projects regarded as unrealistic or fanciful. However, its usage here does not imply acceptance of these pejorative connotations. On the contrary, in my view, utopianism is an essential element in any project for social transformation, including socialism, and today's utopia often becomes tomorrow's reality.

The most obvious common feature in the utopian socialists' transformative projects was the belief that a society based on harmony, association, and cooperation could be established through communal living and working. Such communities were set up in both Europe and America, and although they had mixed success, the most important contribution of the utopians as a whole was their delineation of projects for a new society that were actually put into practice. The utopians' ideas and the communities that attempted to carry them out foreshadowed later forms of socialism. However, those who were the most influential at the time did not necessarily produce the most enduring ideas. In terms of contemporary support, Étienne Cabet was probably the most popular, but his notion of utopia now appears drab.

Cabet (1788–1856) was born in Dijon and, after working as a lawyer, he became a campaigner for workers' rights. In 1834 he was prosecuted

The French social theorist Étienne Cabet (1788–1856) is depicted in this undated lithograph.

for writing an antimonarchist article and was exiled to England for five years. While there he read Thomas More's *Utopia* (1516) and this inspired him to write his own utopian novel, *Voyage to Icaria* (1839). All Icarians were to form "a society founded on the basis of the most perfect equality" with all aspects of life, including clothing, demonstrating these principles. While the degree of regulation and uniformity might now seem repellent, Cabet's Icaria was also highly democratic in terms of the popular participation it envisaged and, at a time when the French working class was suffering from extremes of destitution, it appeared to offer hope for a far better future. With between 100,000 and 200,000 adherents, this was also the most working class of all the utopian socialist movements, attracting fairly low-status artisans, fearful of their position with the development of modern factories. Icarian societies were established all over France, and a group also sailed to America in 1848, with one community remaining there until the end of the nineteenth century. However, while Cabet had considerable contemporary influence, the key utopians in terms of longer-term impact were Henri de Saint-Simon, Charles Fourier, and Robert Owen.

Henri Saint-Simon (1760–1825) was a French aristocrat who defied the conventions of his social class as a student. Imprisoned by his father for refusing to take Communion, he escaped, joined the army, and fought against the British in the American War of Independence. Influenced by the relative absence of social privilege in America, he renounced his title at the beginning of the French Revolution and became convinced that science was the key to progress. His hope, expressed in his *Letters from an Inhabitant of Geneva* (1802–3), was that it would be possible to develop a society based on objective principles. His critique of existing society focused on the continuing semifeudal power relationships in French society rather than on capitalism itself, but his belief in classes as the primary categories of analysis, and his emphasis on the possibility of providing a scientific understanding of historical development, had clear relevance for Marxist theory. However, unlike Marx, he did not see ownership as the most important issue. In his view, history was really based on the rise and fall of different productive and unproductive classes in the various eras. In his own time, he grouped together the overwhelming majority of society—from factory workers to the owners of those factories—as "productive," while the minority of "idlers" (including the nobility and the clergy) were "unproductive." Progress now depended upon the productive classes, the "industrial/scientific class" becoming aware of their mission so that they could effect a transition to the new era. However, this was not simply a replacement of one class by another, as Saint-Simon argued that the industrialists and scientists had a wholly different set of relationships with one another from those between members of the feudal classes. The latter based their position on power, while the industrial/scientific class emphasized cooperation and peaceful competition. The fact that the feudal class still maintained its position was thus a barrier to economic progress and new forms of government.

During his lifetime, Saint-Simon's ideas tended to appeal more to some sectors of the middle classes, who were attracted by the modernizing aspects of the theory, than to the working class, who were perhaps discouraged by his secular tone in a religious age. This was remedied to an extent in his later work, in which he proposed a "religion of Newton," in recognition of Newton's role as the founder of modern science; scientists and artists should head a new church, and he even sought to combine a secular morality with a regenerated form of Christianity, claiming that the main goals were to eradicate poverty and to ensure that all benefited from education and employment. This widened the appeal of his ideas, and immediately after his death Saint-Simonian communities were established in France and elsewhere. Made illegal in France in 1830, they nevertheless continued to have influence up to 1848, with approximately 40,000 adherents. The Saint-Simonian emphasis on industrialism and administrative efficiency as the key to progress and social justice influenced thinking in many other countries, including that of the writer Dostoevsky and other radicals in Russia.

Charles Fourier (1772–1837) also saw himself as a realist, who believed that he had discovered fundamental laws that needed to be implemented to create a new society. However, his ideas were totally different from those of Saint-Simon, and there was a vast gulf between the world he sought to create and his own life. Born in Besançon, the son of a cloth merchant, he lived humbly in boardinghouses and probably never had a sexual relationship. But the utopia that he envisaged, which he called Harmony, was focused on feelings, passions, and sexuality, and perhaps had more points of contact with the movements of the 1960s than with the emerging working class of his own era. Believing that most problems arose from the mismatch between people's passions and the ways in which society functioned, he thought it possible to resolve this conflict through the establishment of so-called phalanxes, or communes. On the basis of a calculation of the number of personality types that he believed to exist, he concluded that just over 1,600 people would be the optimum size of each phalanx, for this would enable all passions to be satisfied and all necessary work to be carried out.

Fourier's basic belief was a conviction that people did not need to change: the problem was the stifling impact of current society, which was the primary cause of human misery. Fourier also condemned the oppression of women, believing this to reveal the malfunctioning of the social system. He did not emphasize the importance of social and economic inequality as a fundamental cause of conflict, assuming that this could be overcome if everybody had a basic minimum, an approach he thought compatible with private property. His comparative lack of interest in the issues of class and inequality meant that Fourierism was the least popular of the movements of early socialists, and there were few factory workers among his followers. But his belief that human unhappiness was caused by psychological and sexual problems and that the remedy lay in changes in society, rather than by treating the individual, certainly anticipated many later forms of socialism.

Like Fourier, Robert Owen (1771–1858) also believed that society, rather than the individual, was responsible for human misery and social ills. But unlike him, Owen believed that people could and should change. The son of a saddler and ironmonger in Wales, he soon revealed an exceptional flair for business, achieving great success in the cotton industry. In 1799 he bought some cotton

The ideas of the Welsh socialist Robert Owen guided the utopian communities of New Lanark, in Scotland, and New Harmony, in Indiana. This statue of Owen stands in Manchester, England.

Robert Owen's experimental settlement at New Lanark in Scotland comprised several buildings on the banks of the River Clyde. This 2009 photograph shows a portion of the fully restored village, now a UNESCO World Heritage Site. Pictured from top left to bottom right are Braxfield Row, a tenement block converted to private houses; mill number three, which now contains a turbine that provides electricity for the village; the Institute for the Formation of Character, now an office building; the school, now a museum; and offices of the Scottish Wildlife Trust. New Lanark is a living and working community and tourist attraction with a resident population of around two hundred.

mills in New Lanark in Scotland, and it was here that he put his ideas into practice.

If Saint-Simon's critique of existing society was based on a kind of class analysis, and Fourier's on the stifling of passions, Owen's owed far more to a condemnation of irrationalism. His enduring belief was in a form of environmental determinism that meant that people were not responsible for their own characters, which were molded by the circumstances in which they lived. In his view, the dominant influences in current society were those of religious dogma and laissez-faire economics. He thought that people would act in superstitious and selfish ways because the whole environment promoted such behavior.

In *A New View of Society* (1813–16) he claimed that, when he arrived at New Lanark, the population

> possessed almost all the vices and very few of the virtues of a social community. Theft and the receipt of stolen goods was their trade, idleness and drunkenness their habit, falsehood and deception their garb; . . . they united only in a zealous systematic opposition to their employers.

In order to change all this, his innovations included the upbringing of children, the approach to crime, the design and location of buildings and leisure facilities, the relationships between the sexes, and the way in which work was organized. His claim was that by introducing such changes, based on the principles of rationality and cooperation, behavior would be transformed.

After sixteen years, a complete change had indeed been brought about in the general character of the village (of approximately two thousand inhabitants) around the mills.

Furthermore, he was quite certain that his principles could be extended to a much wider community and that

> . . . the members of any community may by degrees be trained to live without idleness, without poverty, without crime, and without punishment; for each of these is the effect of error in the various systems prevalent throughout the world. They are all necessary consequences of ignorance.

Viewed in one way, at this stage Owen was an enlightened business entrepreneur, who wanted to increase his own profits by generating more productivity from his workforce. Certainly, his approach was deeply paternalist, and even patronizing, as he talked of inducing good behavior among the "lower orders," and he would continue to reveal such attitudes in later life. But although he sought to convince other employers, the church, and the government of the benefits to be gained by adopting his principles, their response was one of deep hostility. The notion of the perfectability of human beings was held to undermine the Christian belief in original sin, and his emphasis on the social responsibility of employers to their workers was quite out of keeping with the laissez-faire approach of the capitalism of the era.

After failing to win support, his ideas became even more radical and he now attacked the system of private property and profit. In their place he advocated the establishment of new cooperative communities of between 500 and 1,500 people which would combine industrial and agricultural production. He also believed that it would be possible to abolish money and replace it with "labor notes," which would represent the time spent in work and would be exchangeable for goods. By now he was seeking to extend his ideas far beyond Britain, undertaking a continental tour in 1818 and traveling to America, where he established the first of several communities in New Harmony, Indiana, in 1825.

Meanwhile, the London Co-operative Society was also established during the 1820s to promote his thinking and "Exchanges" were set up throughout Britain in which a system of barter took place. Although

This ca. 1825 print is based on English architect Stedman Whitwell's plans for New Harmony, Indiana. The original blueprint noted that the community is "based on the principles advocated by Robert Owen, a socialist philanthropist. The city is designed to give 'greater physical, moral, and intellectual advantages to every individual.' "

these did not meet with great success, by the time he returned to Britain from America in 1829, he had gained a significant level of working-class support, particularly when he joined the movement for trade unionism. However, his influence declined after he broke away from this movement in 1834 and failed to support working-class political demands. His condemnation of the institutions, economic system, and values of contemporary Britain remained wide-ranging, for he continued to argue that these promoted destructive individual self-interest rather than rational cooperation. But he believed that the primary cause was ignorance, rather than malevolence or class interest, and he was often as critical of the workers as the elites. This weakened his appeal at a time when many believed that pressure and conflict would be the only way to bring about change. However, Owen's emphasis on the importance of nurture rather than nature in its widest sense has subsequently been of very considerable influence on a whole range of socialist thought.

Saint-Simon, Owen, and Fourier each presented only a partial critique of existing society, and the same might be said of other early socialists. However, taken together, Saint-Simon's analysis of historical evolution through the category of class, Owen's emphasis on environmental determinism, and Fourier's recognition of the significance of forms of social repression provided important elements in later socialist analyses. The utopian socialists were also conscious of the interconnections between the various dimensions of the problems in existing society. This meant that they did not seek amelioration through partial measures: there needed to be a transformation rather than piecemeal social reform.

Though few of the utopian socialist communities survived beyond the middle of the century, they were of enormous importance in formulating and promoting ideas for a cooperative future society in which ordinary people would play a major role. The utopians made a considerable contribution to socialism by focusing on the specific values of cooperation, association, and harmony in a context of egalitarianism. In the case of Owen and Fourier, this included an emphasis on sexual equality, and there are also some similarities between the utopians' creation of small-scale communities and later ecological thought. They should therefore be regarded as founders of elements of an alternative tradition that would reappear in such communities as the Kibbutz in Palestine/Israel, the communes of the 1960s and 1970s, and in the Green movement; they were progenitors of ideas that would be pursued at the margins for much of the twentieth century.

Anarchism

Anarchism covers a very wide spectrum of opinion, and not all anarchists are socialist in any sense. Here, I will focus on a distinctive form of anarchism which was associated above all with Pierre-Joseph Proudhon (1809–65) and Mikhail Bakunin (1814–76). Apart from reinforcing the utopian vision of decentralized communities, its main contributions to socialism were in its intransigent opposition to the state, and its belief that a revolutionary movement should prefigure the society it wished to create. As will be shown, such views contained a critique of the forms of socialism that would subsequently become dominant.

Like Fourier, Proudhon was born in Besançon in southeastern France and his outlook was essentially rural. However, his fundamental values were in total contrast to those of Fourier: he was antifeminist, antihomosexual, and extremely puritanical. His ideal society remained one in which independent, self-supporting peasants would study and

This photograph of the French philosopher Pierre-Joseph Proudhon (1809–65) was taken in 1862.

live in rather basic conditions. However, in social and political terms he was far more radical than most of the utopian socialists. His phrase, "What is Property? Property is Theft," which first appeared in his pamphlet *What Is Property?* (1840), was one of the best-known revolutionary slogans of the nineteenth century. Here he wrote about government:

> Free association, liberty, limited to maintaining equality in the means of production and equivalence in exchange, is the only possible form of society, the only just and the only true one. Politics is the science of freedom; the government of man by man, under whatever name it is disguised, is oppression: the high perfection of society consists in the union of order and anarchy.

His later works were more complex, but the basic continuity in Proudhon's beliefs was that labor should be the basis for social organization and that all systems of government are oppressive. As he explained in *The Philosophy of Poverty*, if people worked just for themselves and their families, there would be no exploitation because nothing would be produced for employers, who had no real function. The first step for the restoration of healthy economic relations between people was to abolish the whole existing structure of credit and exchange. This would also restore the dignity of labor, currently undermined by machines and the exploitation arising from the capitalist system. Proudhon believed that centralized states and governments were inextricably connected with the economic system, for governments worked hand in hand with the capitalists against ordinary people. When considering the future, he sometimes appeared to believe in a minimal central government formed from delegations from communes, while at other times he envisaged an arrangement whereby a temporary central structure would facilitate the establishment of a new system and then disband. Toward the end of his life, Proudhon devoted his efforts to considering some type of federal system linking the communities. Such ideas represented an attempt to bypass the state by establishing new structures that could carry out all the necessary social functions, thereby rendering the state itself unnecessary. His anarchism had become a real political force among a large section of the working class in France by the 1860s, when the doctrine also entered into the mainstream of European socialism and radicalism. However, it was Bakunin who really challenged Marxism for ascendancy in the developing working-class movements.

Bakunin was born about 150 miles from Moscow into a conservative noble family, but was a constant rebel. He met Proudhon, Marx, and other radical intellectuals in Paris in 1840, and read and discussed current socialist and revolutionary works. However, probably always more interested in action than thought, he became involved in the 1848 revolutions in Europe, securing an international reputation as a result. Bakunin sometimes advocated terror for its own sake and certainly shares some responsibility for anarchism's later association with violence, but his ideas were also important. By now, Marx and Engels had published *The Commu-nist Manifesto* and were endeavoring to influence the European working classes. Some of the key features in Bakunin's thinking were highlighted by his conflicts with the Marxists in the 1860s and early 1870s.

The contribution of Marx and Engels will be explored in the next section, but Bakunin's major disagreements with them can be elucidated here. The first of these concerned their overwhelming emphasis upon the industrial working class in the most advanced capitalist societies as the revolutionary class. Bakunin believed that it was the most oppressed who were potentially the most revolutionary. This meant that revolutionary change was most likely in countries that were the least developed eco-nomically. In his view, Russian peasants were therefore in a strong posi-tion, and he argued that they also had traditional forms of organization in village communal structures that could provide a basis for socialism. Similarly, having spent three years in Italy from 1864 to 1867, he iden-tified great revolutionary potential there because the workers were less privileged and "bourgeois" than elsewhere. Such people, "worn out by . . . daily labor . . . ignorant and wretched," remained "socialist without knowing it" and were "really more socialist than all bourgeois and scien-tific socialists put together."

Bakunin's other major conflict with Marxism focused on issues of organization both before and after the revolution. In 1864 Marx drew up the founding statement for the first socialist international—the Interna-tional Working Men's Association.

Bakunin had joined the International, but then formed a subgroup within it to try to inspire its members with revolutionary fervor. He opposed Marx's idea of creating a (communist) party to win support for socialism, and in 1868 he declared that he hated communism because it is the negation of liberty and because I can conceive nothing human without liberty. I am not a communist because communism concentrates all the powers of society into the state; because it necessarily ends in the centralization of property in the hands of the state, while I want the abolition of the state, which, on the pretext of making men moral and civilized, has up to now enslaved, oppressed, exploited, and depraved them.

Bakunin wanted loosely organized secret societies rather than mass political parties.

The culmination of the conflict between Bakunin and Marx took place in the aftermath of the brutal crushing of the Paris Commune in

The International Working Men's Association was founded in London in 1864. This IWA membership card was signed by officers from several European nations and the United States.

1871, in which workers had taken direct control of affairs in the city, combining legislative and executive power and passing a series of radical measures. Bakunin had taken this as an expression of his own ideas, viewing it as the beginning of a communalist movement which could spread over France as a form of the federalism envisaged by Proudhon. Marx was also deeply influenced and impressed by the Commune. But after its suppression, he believed that it was time to turn the International into a more organized working-class political party. This move was aimed directly at Bakunin, whose influence remained strong, particularly in Spain, Italy, and Switzerland, and anarchism was soon defeated by Marxism as the major influence over European socialist movements.

This engraving, published in 1870, portrays communards—supporters of the revolutionary government during the time of the Paris Commune—erecting a barricade on the rue du Faubourg Saint-Antoine in Paris.

Anarchism would remain important in certain areas—above all, in Spain, until it was crushed by both Franco and the Communists in the Civil War between 1936 and 1939. There and elsewhere it would also coalesce with forms of trade unionism in the syndicalist and anarcho-syndicalist movements, which believed that power could and should be achieved by the workers themselves, rather than through political parties and the state. Like utopian socialism, anarchism also influenced some forms of decentralization and community-based movements from the 1960s. Less positively, during the latter part of the nineteenth century, it often became associated with futile and counterproductive violent acts against individuals—an approach also adopted by some anarchist-inspired groups in late twentieth-century Europe, including the Red Army Faction in the Federal Republic of Germany and the Red Brigades in Italy.

However, the anarchist critique of hierarchical organization remains important. Thus when Marx was attempting to eliminate anarchist influence from the International, some of Bakunin's followers asked:

> How can you expect an egalitarian and free society to emerge from an authoritarian organization? It is impossible. The International, embryo of future human society, must be from this moment the faithful image of our principles of liberty and federation, and reject from its midst any principle leading to authority and dictatorship.

It was certainly a vast exaggeration to suggest that Marx sought to create a dictatorship over the International, or was in a position to do so. But this anarchist cri de coeur would certainly have great relevance in relation to the parties and states created by some of those inspired by Marx in the twentieth century. And, more generally, anarchism provides a perpetual warning for all movements: beware the trappings of power, beware bureaucracy, and ensure that authority is always distrusted. Apart from its vision of decentralized self-governing organizations, this was its essential contribution to socialism.

Karl Marx (1818–83), depicted in this undated engraving, believed that capitalism would eventually be replaced by socialism. His written collaborations with Friedrich Engels are notable not only for their critique of capitalism but also for their repudiation of anarchism and utopianism.

Marxism

The collaboration of Marx (1818–83) and Engels (1820–95) produced the most significant theory in the history of socialism. However, their work has always been open to a variety of interpretations, and dogmatic readings have had greater political resonance than more subtle ones. Since the aim here is to explain the role of Marxism in relation to the evolution of socialist traditions, this section concentrates on its most influential contribution rather than attempting to explore the theory as a whole. In this respect, it is necessary to focus on its critique of capitalism, and its explanation of why this system would eventually be replaced by socialism.

· · · · ·

The partnership between Marx and Engels was one of the most productive in history, but the differences between the two men were remarkable. Marx was the descendant of a line of rabbis on both sides of the family, and his father had only converted to Christianity to maintain his job as a lawyer. Engels was the eldest son of a successful German industrialist who was a fundamentalist Protestant. Marx showed exceptional academic promise and was denied a university career only because of his political views. Engels was forced to join the family firm by his father and was largely self-educated. Marx was untidy, careless about his own appearance, and had almost illegible handwriting. Engels was neat, well organized, smartly dressed, and wrote very clearly. Marx married Jenny von Wesphalen, the daughter of a baron. Engels remained single for most of his life, only marrying Lizzie Burns, a poorly educated working-class woman, on her deathbed in 1878.

Yet from 1844 the two men were political and intellectual collaborators and close friends. Engels has subsequently been overshadowed by Marx; in fact, he said himself that he had always played second fiddle and "been happy to have had such a wonderful first violin as Marx." Certainly, it was an unequal relationship in some respects, with Engels running his family's factory in Manchester in order to support Marx financially while he studied and wrote. Marx was also the more original thinker, but Engels certainly made an indispensable intellectual and political contribution to the partnership.

· · · · ·

The critique of capitalism was embedded in an historical theory (historical materialism) that attempted to explain the whole development of human society. One of Marx and Engels's major criticisms of both the utopian socialists and the anarchists was that they did not deal adequately with the ways in which the present was rooted in the past. Only if these were understood, they believed, was it possible to understand the dynamic processes that would lead to its overthrow. In his *Preface to A Critique of Political Economy* (1859), Marx explained:

> In the social production of their life, men enter into definite relations that are indispensable and independent of their will; these relations of production correspond to a definite stage of development of their material powers of production. The sum total of these relations of production constitutes the economic structure of society—the real foundation, on which rise legal and political superstructure and to which correspond definite forms of social

consciousness. The mode of production in material life determines the general character of the social, political, and spiritual processes of life. It is not the consciousness of men that determines their existence, but, on the contrary, their social existence determines their consciousness.

This passage should not be taken to mean that Marx ignored the whole system of ideas, laws, politics (superstructure), for he examined all this in great detail. But he always related this superstructure to the prevailing economic system. Thus in any social system, such as slave society, feudalism, capitalism, the general ideas and institutions corresponded to the mode of production and were in a sense functional to it. Each system contained a ruling class whose position was derived primarily from controlling the economic surplus, and the dominant ideas and institutions were those that accorded with the interests of that class.

The historical theory also contained a theory of change through revolution. This was never simply identified with a period of violence and, as discussed below, the possibility of peaceful change was not precluded: rather, Marx was arguing that such transformations as those from slave society to feudalism or feudalism to capitalism occurred over long historical eras. However, in the same work he also argued:

At a certain stage of their development the material forces of production in society come into conflict with the existing relations of production, or . . . with the property relations within which they had been at work before. From forms of development of the forces of production these relations turn into their fetters. Then comes the period of social revolution.

For example, while technological advances and improved communications had made it possible for capitalism to develop in feudal Europe, the traditional systems of land ownership and taxation had inhibited those developments. Such structural tensions led to conflicts between the classes that were tied to the different economic systems—the existing feudal structure or the embryonic capitalist (bourgeois) one. These were expressed through political and ideological clashes, culminating in social revolution. Once the rising class had defeated the existing ruling class, it set about transforming the social relationships and superstructure in conformity with the new mode of production.

For socialists, the really important part of the theory was, of course, the critique of capitalism itself and the basis this provided for confidence about its eventual downfall. Again, the theory operated on a number of levels. In *The Communist Manifesto* (1848), Marx and Engels suggested that there were only two antagonistic classes at the heart of the system:

> Our epoch, the epoch of the bourgeoisie, possesses . . . this distinctive feature: it has simplified the class antagonisms. Society as a whole is more and more splitting up into two great hostile camps, into two great classes directly facing each other: Bourgeoisie and Proletariat.

The suggestion was that all other groups (landowners, peasants, artisans) were being squeezed into one or other of these classes. Marx was not always so categorical about this, but certainly argued that it was the contradictory economic interests of these two classes that contained the seeds of destruction of the system.

The starting point for the analysis was a theory of classical political economy: the labor theory of value. The argument here was that the value of a product was determined by the amount of labor that had been necessary to produce it. Marx began with this theory and also thought that in precapitalist societies products had been exchanged because they were useful to the people who bought them. However, he noted that this was not what happened under capitalism: here, the point was to produce commodities which could be exchanged for money and profit. Furthermore, labor had also become a commodity to be bought and sold, but its exchange value was not as great as the exchange value of the product it created. This led Marx (from the 1850s) to argue that it was not labor that created value but labor power. He also introduced the concept of surplus value.

Put simply, his argument was as follows. Those who owned the means of production (for example, factories) sought profit by producing commodities for sale in the market. In the production process, they had two kinds of capital. Marx defined constant capital as "that part of capital . . . transformed into the means of production, that is . . . into raw material, accessory substances, and instruments of labor." In other words, constant capital consisted of such items as materials, machinery, and buildings and it did not change its value during the production process. However, variable capital (labor power) did change value. First, it was able to produce the equivalent of its own value, which, Marx assumed, was normally subsistence for the laborer and their family. If this was, say, $50 per day, the worker would perhaps produce goods of such value within the first four working hours of that day. However, by working for another four hours each day, the laborer could produce double the value (that is, another $50). This would mean that $100 of value had been produced, and the excess between subsistence and the amount taken by capitalists would be the surplus value (in this case $50). Profits came from surplus value, but some expenditure—for example, on new machinery—would also be taken from it. The fundamental economic struggle between labor and capital was over the rate of surplus value (which Marx also called the "rate of exploitation"), with owners of the means of production wanting to increase it and workers to reduce it through higher wages. The consequences of this conflict meant that the capitalist system was prone to crisis.

If surplus value, and therefore profit, was derived only from labor power, there were persistent problems at the heart of the system. Individual capitalists would need to modernize their systems of production through improvements in machinery and technology so as to compete with their rivals. But this meant that they would want to increase their investment in constant capital (machinery) at the expense of labor, which would therefore mean that the share going to labor would decline. However, since surplus value was derived only from variable capital (labor), this meant that there was a long-term tendency for it to fall. The immediate problems could be offset by increasing either the hours of work or the productivity of labor. But, in Marx's view, these were only temporary expedients. Improved production methods meant that more commodities reached the market, but capitalists still needed to keep wages down so as to derive surplus value from each worker. Yet this meant that labor would not have the purchasing power to buy the additional goods and, in this case, production could no longer be profitable. The system would therefore face a crisis of overproduction leading to two results. First, there would be a period of takeovers and mergers as the strongest enterprises forced competitors out of business and effectively destroyed some of the

Marx—and, following him, many socialists throughout history—believed that the proletarian class should unite and press for reforms in order to defeat the capitalist system. This 1895 illustration from the Romanian socialist magazine *Lumea Nouă Ştiinţifică şi Literară* depicts workers' future victory over oppression. In it, a torchbearer wears a sword labeled "Universal Suffrage." She tramples upon four snakes (named Exploitation, Militarism, Corruption, and Ignorance), and leans on a rock labeled "8-hour day." The flag above her says "Proletarians from All Countries Unite." Its green banners proclaim "Brotherhood," "Liberty," and "Justice." One of the books at her feet is Marx's *Das Kapital*; the other announces "Union Makes Strength."

means of production. Second, there would be a depression of wages and the creation of mass unemployment, with increasing poverty and suffering for the proletariat. Eventually, this would lead to a new phase of production in which further capital accumulation based on profits derived from surplus value would again be possible, but the same structural problems would remain, and new crises were endemic in the system. Moreover, each crisis would tend to be more severe than the previous one, eventually leading to the breakdown of the system itself.

Marx appeared to be saying something very categorical: that the position of the proletariat was becoming ever more wretched and that the downfall of capitalism was inevitable. In fact, he may have been less certain about the absolute decline in working-class living standards than it often appeared; he also believed that trade unionism and reforms could lead to definite improvements in the situation of the workers and that "subsistence" was an historical concept, the content of which would be affected by evolving conceptions of the minimum acceptable standard of living with economic and technological development. Similarly, despite rhetoric that sometimes implied that the collapse of capitalism was imminent, elsewhere he suggested that it would take a very long time to exhaust all its possibilities of expansion. Yet the notion of eventual breakdown was embedded in both Marx's materialist conception of history and in his political economy of capitalism.

The seeds of transformation were inherent within the operation of the existing system, which was never static. The future was not to be created by establishing communities practicing a new system, as the utopian socialists had believed, or by a group of people "smashing the state," as in some anarchist visions. However, Marx certainly did not believe that everything was determined by structural forces. On the contrary, political activity by the proletariat was essential. Its growing class consciousness also meant a developing awareness of the bourgeoisie as both separate and antagonistic. From this, socialist and revolutionary consciousness would also emerge over time. Thus the structural features of capitalism created an objective antagonism between the two fundamental classes within it; but the development and operation of the system then produced the kind of subjective consciousness that would ultimately lead to a revolutionary process, focusing on the capture of state power.

This followed from Marx and Engels's theory of the origins of the state. This, it was argued, had really developed only with the earliest division of labor, which had itself arisen once society had been able to produce a surplus off which some people could live without contributing directly to producing the means of life for the whole community. Thereafter, the state had primarily been an instrument to serve the interests of the dominant class in each social system. The most famous expression of this viewpoint was in the claim in *The Communist Manifesto* that "the executive of the modern state is but a committee for managing the common affairs of the whole bourgeoisie." This no doubt overstated Marx and Engels's position, but expressed the essence of their theory. The state, the dominant ideology, the legal system, and a host of other institutions combined to serve the interests of the bourgeoisie and to uphold the capitalist system. Thus the critique of the existing system included its political institutions, for these served the interests that oppressed the overwhelming majority of the population.

The emphasis of Marx's writings and speeches suggested that revolutionary change would involve violence. Yet he was also critical of those who equated revolution with insurrection or a coup by an organized group. Marx's point was that the revolutionary crisis was the culmination of a much longer evolutionary process within the existing society. This meant that a premature attempt to bring about revolutionary change could not succeed, and he criticized the violence of the most radical elements (the Jacobins) in the French Revolution, arguing that this had followed from the attempt to impose conditions for which society was not yet ready. In 1848, and at the time of the Paris Commune in 1871, he appeared to accept the need for violence, but at other times he urged the path of reform. He even held out the possibility of peaceful revolution, suggesting that Britain, the USA, and Holland might possess the appropriate conditions for this to take place. After Marx's death, Engels seemed more decided on this path, working with the German Sozialdemokratische Partei Deutschlands (SPD), on practical programs for reform.

The other general element in Marx and Engels's conception of revolutionary change concerned the role of the working class and of a political party. They seem to have taken it for granted that the development of class consciousness led, almost automatically, as they put it in *The Communist Manifesto*, to the "organization of the proletarians into a class, and consequently into a political party." In other words, the implication was that the proletariat was only a class in a full sense when it was conscious of itself as such, and at this point it also turned itself into a political party. The working class was thus the agent in the revolutionary process and a political party would be its instrument in this struggle. But Marx and Engels were not at all categorical as to when or how this kind of transformation would come about.

Marx and Engels revolutionized thinking about society, transcending conventional boundaries between fact and value, and between philosophy, history, economics, sociology, and politics. As an explanation of historical change, an analysis of the dynamics of capitalism, and a prognosis about the role of the working class as an agency for transcending that system, Marx and Engels's work expressed theoretical insights that far surpassed those of their predecessors. It is also worth noting that when, in his *Critique of the Gotha Program* (1875), Marx discussed the features of a postrevolutionary society, he was rather cautious about the extent of progress, particularly in relation to equality, that could be made "in the first phase of communist society." It was only in the higher phase that society could "inscribe on its banners: from each according to his ability, to each according to his needs!" His explanation of the transition from the first to the second stage may not be entirely convincing, but, despite the rhetorical flourishes in some of their work, Marx and Engels were providing a general approach to analysis rather than a set of "right answers." Yet to acknowledge the crucial importance of their insights is not to suggest that they were entirely valid in their own time—let alone in the twenty-first century—and elements of the theory will be discussed later in the book.

Social Democracy Before 1914

By 1883, when Marx died, the major features of socialist ideas had been established. Utopian socialists, anarchists, and Marxists had many crucial points of disagreement, but there was a common emphasis on equality, cooperation, and social solidarity. All also stressed their commitment to the poorer social strata, although it was only with Marx that a specific theory of class and class conflict had crystallized. However, it was after his death that the final forms of modern socialism emerged, with the dominance of political parties.

Between the 1880s and the outbreak of the First World War, there was a massive growth in socialist parties in Europe, all of which came together in the Second International, founded in 1889. However, these parties were ambiguous in various ways. In the first place, their names, confusing at the time, have become much more so in the light of later developments. For although they were collectively known as socialist parties when meeting in the International, and most of them professed the goal of socialism, only a minority used the term in their own names. Some used "workers" or "labor," but the most common title was "social democratic party." Communist parties did not yet exist and social democracy covered a spectrum of views, including those that would later identify themselves with communism. With the formation of communist parties after the First World War, social democrats and communists would become bitter antagonists and, in the process, social democracy would change.

With the British Labour Party as the only important exception, all these parties owed their doctrinal inspiration to the Marxist critique of capitalism. The SPD was easily the largest party in the International and was the most dominant intellectually. During these years, Karl Kautsky (1854–1938) became the most influential interpreter of Marxist doctrine, not only in the German Social Democratic Party, but in the International as a whole. Having lived in London for much of the 1880s, he became quite close to Engels and this reinforced his credentials as the authentic voice of Marxism. However, he tended to interpret it in a rather mechanical way, emphasizing the inevitability of the eventual triumph of socialism. His position also epitomized the difficulties of attempting to reconcile a revolutionary doctrine with electoral and parliamentary politics and incorporated the key tensions between reform and revolution that characterized the International as a whole.

The SPD's program was agreed at Erfurt in 1891 and, as Donald Sassoon has argued, two aspects coexisted within it with rather tenuous

The German chancellor Otto von Bismarck introduced an anti-socialist law that banned the German socialist party, or SPD, from 1878 to 1890. This cartoon, drawn by the artist Edward Linley Sambourne and published in an 1878 issue of the British magazine *Punch*, portrays Bismarck trying to force the socialist "Jack" back into his box.

links between them. The first part was an orthodox Marxist summary of the situation, stressing the division of society into two hostile camps, with fewer large-scale capitalist enterprises constantly expanding their control over the economic system, ever more serious crises of overproduction, and the necessity for the SPD to acquire political power so as to establish a socialist system based on common ownership. The second part concentrated on a series of measures that appeared to constitute a program of reform within the system, rather than its total transformation. There were always different shades of opinion within the party, but the general agreement was that this was a program that combined immediate benefits for the proletariat with the long-term goal of socialism. In other words, it was generally seen as both a reformist and revolutionary program, with reforms sought within capitalism—not as a substitute for revolution, but as a means toward it. This was the dominant interpretation within the SPD and more widely within the Second International.

By 1914, the emergence of parties with a form of Marxist theory as the dominant ideology seeking mass membership and majority electoral support had already pushed alternative socialist traditions to the margins. This did not mean that there were no challengers. For example, in the years immediately before the war there was a sharp increase in militant rank-and-file strikes in several European countries. This reflected a belief (often defined as syndicalism) that direct industrial action, rather than working through political parties, was the way to achieve change and construct a new society. Yet it was already evident that these were alternative rather than mainstream positions.

One further element in the newly dominant tradition of socialism was its professed acceptance of working-class internationalism. It was generally understood that all the parties shared the view that the workers had no country because their common enemy was capitalism. Hence all of them agreed—in theory—that they would be totally opposed to a capitalist war. None of them, it was constantly asserted, would support their own governments should such a war break out. In reality, most of them did just this in 1914. This certainly increased the divisions within the parties, with an active minority opposing both the mainstream leadership and the war yet. It may have been possible

One of the tenets of the early socialists was that the goals of all workers—equality, fair pay, freedom from tyranny—cut across national boundaries. The lyrics to the anthem "L'Internationale," originally written by Eugène Pottier in 1871, and later set to music by Pierre De Geyter in 1888, were translated into many languages, and it is sung throughout the world to this day. The artist Théophile-Alexandre Steinlen (1858–1923) created the cover art for this edition of the anthem's sheet music in 1902.

to reconstruct the International after the war had it not been for the Bolshevik (communist) Revolution in 1917.

The Emergence of Communism

Modern communism was created with the assumption of power in Russia by the Bolshevik party. Subsequently, the new rulers claimed that the party represented the authentic application of Marxism in the contemporary era, and implied that there was continuity between themselves and nineteenth-century communists. In fact, the relationship between Bolshevism and Marxism remains highly controversial and the idea of continuity is very dubious. There was no clear distinction between communism and socialism for most of the previous century. At times, the term communism had implied a more revolutionary approach to bringing about change, and this impression was perhaps reinforced when Marx and Engels published *The Communist Manifesto* in 1848. But the manifesto was written for the so-called Communist League, a group of émigré German workers that soon faded away, and the terms "socialist" and "communist" were not even used consistently by Marx and Engels.

In any case, according to all the guardians of orthodoxy, Russia should not have been the location for the first Marxist-inspired revolution, for the peasantry formed the overwhelming majority of the population and serfdom had only been abolished as recently as 1861. The idea that the revolution would first occur in an advanced capitalist country had been emphasized by Marx and Engels and embedded in the thinking of the socialists of the Second International. Until 1914, Russian Marxists had generally shared this view and had tended to defer to Kautsky, the main theorist of the German SPD, on many issues of doctrine. However, developments that had already taken place in the Russian party, along with the crisis over the war, now combined to transform the situation.

The Russian Social-Democratic Labor Party had been formed in 1899 as the main organizational focus for Russian Marxists. However, it had soon dissolved into factions, one of which had been led by Vladimir Lenin (1870–1924). Because of his energy, clarity, and revolutionary commitment, he had soon emerged as a leading figure, and in *What Is to Be Done?* (1902) he proposed that a wholly new type of party should be established. This proved highly divisive at the Party Congress in 1903, and brought about a split, with the Bolsheviks now effectively operating as a separate party even before the final break in 1912. Lenin (and the Bolsheviks more generally) was totally opposed to socialists in any part of the world who supported the war. He denounced them in the most bitter terms and sought (unsuccessfully) to persuade dissident socialists to turn the international war into a revolutionary war in their own countries. The Bolshevik seizure of power transformed the power relationships within the international socialist movement. The Bolsheviks changed their name to the Communist Party soon after the revolution (the term "Bolshevik" had simply meant "majority"), and Moscow became the center of the doctrine that now became known as communism. It is therefore necessary to consider some of its main features in Russia around the time of the revolution.

Lenin returned to Russia from exile in April 1917, a month after the first revolution that had overthrown the Tsar and brought a provisional government to power, with Alexander Kerensky (1881–1970) at its head. Soviets (workers' councils) had also been established in the major cities, demanding food and peace but, under pressure from Britain and France, Kerensky was insisting on continuing with the war. Although it

This colorized photograph of Vladimir Lenin (1870–1924) was taken around the time of the second congress of the Communist International, or Comintern, in 1920. The congress institutionalized the split between communism and social democracy.

was obvious that the majority of the population was desperate to end the fighting, most of the Bolsheviks still believed that it was impossible for a socialist revolution to take place in a backward country. It took Lenin's personal ascendancy to convince them that a successful revolution was indeed possible in Russia and that this would then be followed by revolutions elsewhere. In these circumstances, the hope was that like-minded governments in more advanced countries would then help the development of socialism in Russia. With the slogans of "all power to the Soviets" and "bread, land and peace," the Bolsheviks secured a majority in the Soviets and achieved a revolutionary insurrection that enabled them to take control in a situation where there was, in effect, a power vacuum.

Shortly before the seizure of power, Lenin had written *The State and Revolution*, which had been wildly optimistic about the way in which socialism could be established after a revolution. The reality was quite different, for the Bolsheviks were now faced with four tasks that were not easily reconcilable. First, they had to establish themselves in power when they had only a minority of support in the country. Second, they needed to implement measures that would demonstrably change social relationships in a rigidly authoritarian society based on traditional hierarchies. Third, they needed to maintain the temporary alliance between the peasantry and the urban proletariat that had enabled them to seize control. Fourth, they needed to bring about massive economic growth so as to improve living standards. It is perhaps hardly surprising that they failed, particularly as their more positive aims were necessarily subordinated, until the end of 1920, to the urgent task of winning a civil war. However, the situation led to a particular form of authoritarian socialism becoming increasingly marked.

Even after the Bolsheviks had taken over, they talked of a democratically elected Constituent Assembly as the body that would rule, and they clearly expected to win a majority there. However, when the election results in January 1918 showed that they had won only 21% of the seats, they dissolved the Assembly. As far as Lenin was concerned, the situation by then was such that the only alternatives were Bolshevik rule or rule by the extreme Right, and he was not willing to risk the latter. It is quite probable that his analysis of the situation was valid, but the decision obviously had important political implications. It soon led to a situation in which the communists were dominating all organs of power and, by the end of the civil war, the party and the Red Army had become increasingly autocratic. Each new extension of power was justified as a temporary measure, but the party/state dictatorship was now being constructed.

At the beginning, severe repression in some spheres (for example, against religion) was coupled with a real attempt to open up culture, spread educational opportunities, and bring about sexual equality. But as early as December 1917, the Cheka (or secret police) was established to discover and suppress any attempts at counterrevolution. It used summary executions and imprisonment against any suspects—some of whom were regarded as such simply because of their social origins. After an attempt on Lenin's life in May 1918, the Red Terror was promulgated, leading to thousands of executions and the Cheka operating almost as a state within the state. By 1920, the economy was also destitute after six years of war, the support of the peasantry was in danger of being lost completely, and some eight million people had died from disease and malnutrition since the Bolshevik Revolution.

The Break Between Communism and Social Democracy

While many European socialists were exhilarated by the first Marxist-inspired revolution, others were less convinced. As they watched the dissolution of the Constituent Assembly, the revolutionary terror, and the evolution toward a one-party state, their doubts as to whether this was really socialism increased. In some cases, particularly among the leaders of West European socialist parties, such sentiments were probably reinforced when they heard themselves denounced as traitors and renegades by the Soviet leaders. Other Western socialists were prepared to accept that such harsh measures might be necessary in Russian conditions, where there had been no tradition of democracy and where counterrevolutionaries also used terror as a political weapon, but they did not believe that they could be justified in countries where peaceful change through constitutional means might be possible. Others went further than this and questioned whether the Bolshevik Revolution could even be justified in Marxist terms. One of the most powerful arguments of this kind was put forward in December 1920 at a Congress of the French Socialist Party.

The Congress was held at Tours to decide whether or not the party should affiliate to the new Communist International. Léon Blum (1872–1950), who would become prime minister in the French Popular Front government in 1936, was the leader of one of the groups that were totally opposed to affiliation. In his speech, he claimed that the dictatorship in Russia stemmed from its conception of revolution. Instead of a seizure of power following a long period of evolution creating the preconditions for socialism, it had been interpreted in terms of insurrection by a small group, who then needed to create those preconditions. Whereas the Marxist conception was of a temporary impersonal dictatorship based on mass support, the Bolshevik one was of semipermanent dictatorship exercised by a centralized and hierarchical party. Blum was thus implying either that socialism could not be established in this way, or that the only form of socialism that would emerge was one that negated its own ideals because it was inherently undemocratic. However, he was defeated at the Congress, where there was considerable enthusiasm for the Russian Revolution, and the majority now formed the French Communist Party.

The fissure that opened up between communism and social democracy developed in the aftermath of the Bolshevik Revolution, but it is also necessary to appreciate some aspects of Lenin's thinking that had been revealed even before 1914 and which were institutionalized after the revolution. The most fundamental element in all this was his absolute and total commitment to the goal of socialist revolution. This underlay his whole strategic and tactical approach, including important innovations. For example, Marxists had normally tended to regard the urban working class as the vehicle for socialist revolution and had been rather indifferent to the peasantry and to the forces of nationalism. However, Lenin had understood that a revolution could take place in Russia only on the basis of alliances with the peasantry (the overwhelming mass of the population) and the numerous subject nationalities that sought liberation from rule by the Russian majority. But it was Lenin's belief in the necessity for a particular kind of party to hasten the revolutionary process that was of particular relevance for the subsequent split with social democracy.

Lenin put forward his idea of a vanguard party, based on revolutionaries fighting a class war in the same way that the military fought a conventional war. This differed from anything suggested by Marx and Engels for, although they had taken it for granted that a party would be necessary, they had also insisted that the working class would emancipate itself. However, Lenin now argued that, left to itself, the working class would develop "trade union" consciousness, but not revolutionary consciousness. In other words, conflicts over pay and working conditions would inevitably arise, but the workers would not themselves locate these issues within a wider Marxist framework. Because workers would remain integrated within the dominant ideological framework, it was necessary for revolutionary socialist consciousness to be brought to them by a vanguard party that did understand Marxist theory, whose members would tend to be bourgeois intellectuals. This was obviously an extremely contentious notion. Lenin might argue that this was not party control over the workers because it would be working with them, but there were certainly elements of elitism: the workers had a false consciousness that must be redirected by those with superior understanding.

The serious implications of this notion were reinforced by Lenin's ideas about party organization, for all the emphasis was upon secrecy, centralization, and professional revolutionaries. Some of his thinking was certainly shaped by the need to operate in clandestine conditions during the Tsarist autocracy, which he contrasted with the relatively open conditions in Germany. Yet he slid from a discussion about the Russian situation to far more general notions, which implied that centralism and secrecy were more important to him than democracy. Furthermore, the very idea of a party leadership having the right to impose a single view on its members was highly questionable. The result was surely bound to be one in which policy directives became diktats, with most members simply having to take it on trust that decisions had been arrived at through discussion and debate. This was compounded by the fact that the party discourse under Lenin was always based on binary alternatives: a given idea or policy was either bourgeois or socialist—shades of gray did not exist.

Although many commentators have tended to regard the Leninist party as pivotal for the subsequent establishment of the dictatorship by Stalin (1879–1953), it can equally well be argued that he destroyed and bypassed it. Many revolutionary Marxists, who are highly critical of the direction taken by the Soviet Union, therefore continue to believe that the Leninist conception of the party, based on the system of "democratic centralism," was valid and the problems only developed with later applications of that conception. Yet it is notable that two of the most eminent Marxist revolutionaries of the era had themselves criticized Lenin's notion of the vanguard party when it had first been formulated.

The Polish-born German philosopher Rosa Luxemburg was murdered after being arrested during an abortive revolutionary uprising. A theoretician and activist, she had unshakable faith in the revolutionary and democratic potential of the working class and was critical of both German social democracy and Bolshevism.

Rosa Luxemburg (1871–1919) was a revolutionary Marxist in the German SPD. She was often deeply critical of the leadership of her own party because she believed it was becoming too dominated by short-term reforms and was losing sight of the ultimate goal of socialist revolution. However, she believed in mass action by the working class as the way of bringing about change and was critical of Lenin's concept of a vanguard party. In 1903, she attacked it for ultra-centralism, which she equated with the "sterile spirit of the overseer":

> Lenin's concern is not so much to make the activity of the party more fruitful as to control the party—to narrow the movement rather than to develop it, to bind rather than unify it.

Once the Russian Revolution took place, she gave it cautious support and was a leading figure in the German Communist Party when it was established in December 1918. However, the next month she (and Karl Liebknecht, another prominent figure in the new party) were arrested by German cavalry officers, who were suppressing a revolutionary uprising. Both were murdered while in custody, so Luxemburg did not live to witness the subsequent development of the Soviet system and the uses that would be made of the Leninist party.

The other early critic was Leon Trotsky (1879–1940). When Lenin developed his concept of the party, Trotsky had not supported him, but subsequently he changed his mind and became a leading figure in the revolution of 1917 and the postrevolutionary regime. When Lenin died in January 1924, Trotsky was one of the two most probable successors, but he was out-maneuvered by Stalin, who expelled him from the Soviet Union in 1929. In exile, he denounced the betrayal of revolution and sought to revive the original spirit of Bolshevism as he interpreted it. As a result, he was assassinated by Stalin's agents in Mexico in 1940.

Trotsky always insisted that there was no basis for Stalinism in Lenin's concept of the party, and this view has generally been taken by the Trotskyist parties that subsequently developed in many parts of the world. However, his initial verdict on the idea could be taken as a prediction of the methods that Stalin would later use and from which Trotsky himself would suffer. In 1904 he thus wrote:

The Russian politician Leon Trotsky (1879–1940), shown in this undated photograph, was exiled by Stalin in 1929 and killed in Mexico by one of Stalin's agents in 1940. He continues to inspire many revolutionary Marxists.

In inner-party politics, these methods [of Lenin] lead, as we shall yet see, to this: the party organization substitutes itself for the party, the Central Committee substitutes itself for the organization, and finally, a "dictator" substitutes himself for the Central Committee.

The origins of Bolshevik party organization, lay in Russian conditions, but by 1919 the situation had been transformed. Convinced that a revolution could occur elsewhere—and particularly in Germany—if the organizational and ideological features of Bolshevism were adopted, the model was now imposed on all parties seeking to join the new Communist International (the Comintern) created in Moscow. The entry conditions required all who joined to accept the doctrine and practices of the Bolsheviks in their own parties and, in effect, the Comintern itself also sought to replicate this organizational principle, with the policies of the individual parties largely determined by the Executive Committee. This notion of a centrally controlled, vanguard revolutionary party was distasteful to socialists with a belief in reform and democracy. Thus when the Comintern insisted that this model must be imposed on all member parties, with the policies of each communist party determined by the Executive Committee, the break with social democracy was clear.

Yet it would be wrong to attribute responsibility for the break entirely to Lenin and the Bolsheviks, for the Marxist terminology of Second International socialism had also masked a tendency that now became much stronger: the pursuit of socialism through constitutional means. Before the war, only the British Labour Party had explicitly avowed constitutional politics as the sole means to bring about change, and it had also concentrated on practical reforms rather than discussions of ultimate goals. Elsewhere, it had generally been maintained that the achievement of reforms was just one element in a Marxist revolutionary strategy. While there was room for considerable skepticism as to whether this was, in fact, what the parties were practicing, the official claim had just about survived intact until 1914. Thereafter, their support for the war had exposed the gap between rhetoric and reality. Moreover, the performance of some of the parties after the fighting ended confirmed the view that working within the system would supersede any previous claims that the objective was to overthrow it through extra-parliamentary activity. The most notorious instance of this was the SPD's collaboration with the old elites to establish the Weimar Republic in 1919 rather than to support those who were attempting to overthrow capitalism through revolution. It is highly unlikely that a revolution could have succeeded, but the caution of the SPD leadership was widely criticized both at the time and subsequently. Its reliance on paramilitary forces was to make the break between social democracy and communism particularly bitter in Germany. However, the more general point is that after 1920 a new form of social democracy emerged that had effectively abandoned the idea of seeking socialism through a revolutionary seizure of power.

Many of the parties still used Marxist discourse and attempted to justify their policies in relation to the ultimate goal of revolution. Some breakaway parties even fought bravely to find a "third way" between communism and social democracy in the so-called Vienna (or second-and-a-half) International, before abandoning the attempt in 1923. However, this was much less significant than the fact that the parties that then formed the Labor and Socialist International concentrated primarily on seeking power through parliamentary means and advocating practical reforms, with the British Labour Party entering the mainstream of social democracy. This does not mean that they no longer aspired to establish socialism by abolishing capitalism, but there was now an absolute division between social democracy and communism. Communists were institutionally part of the Comintern and sought to emulate Soviet theory and practice. Social democrats rejected the Soviet model and effectively accepted the notion that there was some convergence between their own views and those of others, such as left-wing liberals, who believed in parliamentary democracy and social reform. Two kinds of political parties, allegedly serving the interests of the working classes, had become the main agencies for the establishment of socialism, and these two traditions now struggled for ascendancy in Europe and the rest of the world.

TWO

Cuban Communism and Swedish Social Democracy

•

Developments in Communism and Social Democracy

The fissure between communism and social democracy that developed in the aftermath of the Bolshevik Revolution never really healed. Certainly, there were times—particularly between 1935 and 1939 and between 1941 and 1945—when it seemed that common opposition to fascism might transcend the divisions of the Left. There were also some countries—for example, Italy during the early postwar period— where there was considerable support for unity. However, in general,

Cuban communism—and its long history of achievements and disappointments—provides an instructive model for those seeking to understand how socialism can grow in a world dominated by capitalist markets. This undated photograph shows the Cuban flag hanging on the side of an old building in Havana.

communists and social democrats remained in separate and hostile camps, particularly at the height of the cold war. Yet neither tradition was monolithic or unchanging.

In general, social democratic parties experienced persistent difficulties in self-definition after the break with communism. As most of them had claimed to be Marxist before 1914, and had disputed the communist appropriation of the doctrine in the early postwar period, it was difficult simply to abandon it thereafter. On the other hand, it was clear that they accepted liberal democratic institutions as the primary route through which to implement changes. Some parties, particularly those competing for the allegiance of the working class with a large communist party, continued to claim Marxism as a doctrinal source long after it ceased to play an important role in influencing policy. The French Socialist Party was particularly prone to this. Thus Léon Blum, still facing the pre-1914 problem as to whether a socialist party could participate in a bourgeois coalition, distinguished between "the exercise of power" (participation in government) and "the conquest of power" (overthrow of capitalism). Yet although his Popular Front government in 1936 implemented some important reforms immediately after coming to power, its subsequent economic policy was very orthodox and unimaginative. In Germany, the situation of the SPD was to become more catastrophic. Despite its preeminent role in establishing the liberal-democratic system in 1919 and remaining committed to it during the years of acute instability until 1923, the party was then normally excluded from power, although it secured the largest share of the vote until 1930. In 1928 the SPD's success in the elections made it impossible to form a cabinet without it, but it would not agree to the cut in unemployment benefit sought by its partners. The result was the effective abolition of the parliamentary system and rule by decree from 1930. The bitter division between the SPD and the Communist Party then prevented a united front against Nazism, though both parties were immediate victims after Hitler's takeover of power in 1933. The SPD had wanted to uphold the democratic system and remained committed to constitutionalism even when it was increasingly evident that its opponents supported dictatorship. But it never formulated a program of reform to resolve the economic crisis after 1929, tending to share the communist belief that this was the final collapse of capitalism. The SPD represented interwar social democracy in its most tragic form. However, the difficulties were not confined to the parties that still claimed a Marxist influence. Neither of the brief attempts of the British Labour Party to wield power through minority governments in the interwar period was notably successful. In particular, its failure to deal with the economic depression in 1931, and the decision of its leader and then prime minister, Ramsay MacDonald (1866–1937), to head a Conservative-dominated coalition in order to implement austerity measures, led to the worst crisis the party ever faced. Confined to opposition for the rest of the interwar period, it was divided and relatively impotent until it joined the wartime coalition led by Winston Churchill.

The raison d'être of social democracy after the split with communism had been the claim that socialism could be implemented peacefully. However (with the notable exception of Sweden), the general experience of the interwar period was one of clear failure. Most capitalist societies experienced either serious economic depression, characterized by mass unemployment and a reduction in social expenditure or, still worse, the elimination of liberal-democracy and its replacement by extreme rightwing dictatorship. Such outcomes clearly constituted a practical and intellectual defeat for the project of social democracy. For it had certainly not demonstrated its ability to eliminate poverty and create a more equal society imbued with the values of cooperation and solidarity. Subsequently, both the nature of social democracy and the problems it faced underwent further changes.

During the interwar period, the only major liberal-democratic country that had successfully implemented practical measures to revive the economy and create jobs had been the USA, under President Roosevelt and the New Deal. However, Roosevelt was not a socialist, but a pragmatic American Democrat. Similarly, the foremost economist, who had explained in theoretical terms how a government could stimulate economic expansion during a depression, had been John Maynard Keynes (1883–1946), a British Liberal. So neither the practical nor the theoretical originators of the reforms underlying postwar capitalism were from the social democratic tradition. But when "Keynesian" economics was put into practice between the late 1940s and the early 1970s, there was a prolonged period of economic growth, leading to far higher living standards in Western Europe, and a much greater proportion of GNP devoted to welfare expenditure, than ever before. But this raised new questions for social democracy: had capitalism been changed by social democracy so that its values were now incorporated in the system? Or had capitalism in advanced industrial countries become so successful that it could now afford concessions to the working classes whether or not these were demanded by social democracy? Naturally, the parties sought to convince their electorates that they had brought about the changes but, paradoxically, it could also be argued that one of the main factors underpinning the development of welfare capitalism in the postwar era was the role of the USA in the cold war. In any case, the more relevant point was the impact of these changes on the nature of social democracy.

This portrait of the British economist John Maynard Keynes (1883–1946) was taken in the late 1930s by the photographer Gorden Anthony.

As social expenditure increased and full employment was established, most social democratic parties underwent a further evolution. Most now became more openly committed to the goal of progressive social reform, rather than the total elimination of the capitalist system. This was not a smooth or uniform process, for the parties contained minorities that adhered to a more traditional version of socialism. Some parties even insisted that they had not changed. Certainly, important differences remained between them, with variations in ideology, relationships with trade unions, and the social composition of the members and supporters of the parties. Yet social democracy could now be characterized as a tradition seeking to promote increasing benefits for the working classes within a primarily capitalist system. The fact that control over much of the economy remained in private hands inevitably limited the power of social democracy and further constraints stemmed from its need to secure electoral support for its measures.

Communism also evolved after the break with social democracy. After 1917, communist parties were established throughout the world but, until the end of the Second World War, communism was inseparable from the Soviet experience. For it was only there that a communist regime was in power, and the other parties demonstrated their allegiance to it. However, after the Second World War, the communist movement gradually became less monolithic and Soviet control was reduced. The leader of Yugoslavia, Josip Broz Tito (1892–1980), had a serious dispute with Stalin and had broken away from the Soviet bloc by 1948. The system he established was based on one-party rule, but with far greater decentralization of the economy than in the Soviet Union. Of greater importance, in 1949 the Chinese Communist Party under Mao Zedong (1893–1976) finally achieved power after more than twenty years of revolutionary struggle and civil war. The Chinese system differed very considerably from the Soviet model, with much more emphasis on the continuing role of the peasantry. Furthermore, by the 1960s relations between China and the Soviet Union had become so poor that border clashes took place and a war seemed possible. This also led to divisions within the international communist movement, and some now turned to Maoism for their inspiration (as the revolutionaries in Nepal still do). Other communist regimes had been established in North Korea, following a division in the country after the Second World War; in Vietnam (initially in the north of the country, but throughout the whole state in 1975 following the withdrawal of the U.S. after a prolonged war); and in Cuba, following the revolution in 1959.

Greater diversity in communism also followed from revelations made by the Soviet leader Nikita Krushchev (1894–1971) at the Soviet Party Congress in 1956. There he denounced aspects of Stalin's rule and presented some of the evidence about the atrocities that had taken place. This led some West European communist parties (particularly those in Italy and Spain) gradually to move away from Soviet control and, during the 1970s, to proclaim the doctrine of Eurocommunism. In this they declared their acceptance of a multiparty system, free speech, and many characteristics of liberal democracy. But, despite their many differences, all communist states maintained a single-party system, substantial state ownership of the economy, an adherence to an official ideology based on an interpretation of Marxism, and the maintenance of power through nondemocratic means.

Commentary on both communism and social democracy has tended to be dominated by a concentration upon the biggest powers: the Soviet Union and China in relation to communism; and Germany, Britain, and

France in relation to social democracy. While this is certainly justifiable in the sense that world history is dominated by the big battalions, it can also lead to unjustifiably negative conclusions about socialism. This is particularly obvious in respect of the Soviet Union and China, where the very scale of violence and repression makes it difficult to scrutinize the costs and benefits of the regimes in a dispassionate way. The failings of social democratic governments in the large European states bear no comparison with the crimes of Stalinism or Maoism, but it is difficult to argue that they ever created an alternative model of society reflecting socialist values. While no party has been entirely successful in this respect, Swedish social democracy and Cuban communism both attempted to implement the goals of equality, cooperation, and solidarity and both demonstrated significant achievements. It is for this reason that these two states have been selected as case studies.

However, in presenting these case studies side by side, I am not suggesting symmetry between them. The important differences between communism and social democracy that emerged after the Bolshevik Revolution affected the ideological universe of each, particularly in relation to such key issues as democracy and private ownership. The environments in which they have operated have also been quite different. In 1959 (the year of the Cuban revolution) Swedish social democrats had the comparative luxury of living in a wealthy and stable liberal-democracy facing no significant external threat, while the dominating preoccupations for Fidel Castro were the poverty of the island and its extreme vulnerability to attack by a bitterly hostile superpower just across the water. Nevertheless, there are also some interesting points of comparison, for both Swedish social democrats and Cuban communists have tried to bring about significant social changes in a world dominated by much larger powers, and both have been increasingly constrained by changes in the wider international political economy.

Swedish Social Democracy

Origins and Characteristics of the Swedish Model

The Swedish Social Democratic Party (*Socialdemokratiska Arbetarpartiet*, or SAP) paid formal obeisance to Marxism before 1914, but there were some strongly revisionist overtones in both its rhetoric and formal statements even then. Moreover, Hjalmar Branting, who dominated the party from 1900 until 1925, had originally been a liberal and, particularly in his later years, sought to effect a synthesis between liberalism and socialism.

Another important figure, Per Albin Hansson, who became the first SAP prime minister in 1932, made a frequently quoted statement that characterized a further key aspect in Swedish social democracy—the *folkhemmet*, or conception of society and the state as the "people's home":

> The basis of the home is togetherness and common feeling. The good house does not consider anyone either as privileged or unappreciated; it knows no special favorites or stepchildren. There no one looks down upon anyone else, there no one tries to gain advantage at another's expense, and the stronger do not suppress and plunder the weaker. In the good home equality, consideration, cooperation, and helpfulness prevail. Applied to the great people's and citizens' home this would mean the breaking down of all the social and economic barriers that now divide citizens into the privileged and the unfortunate, into rulers and subjects. . . .

In its unbroken period of rule from 1932 until 1976, the SAP introduced a series of major and enduring economic and social reforms that
were broadly in harmony with these sentiments.

A further characteristic of Swedish social democracy was the fact
that it rested as much on trade unionism, and particularly the blue-collar

Every four years, the Swedish people elect 349 representatives to their riksdag, or parliament.
The room in which the parliament meets appears in this recent photograph.

confederation, the LO (*Landsorganisationen*), as on the party. This, of course, was not unique to Sweden, for there was also an organic relationship between British trade unionism and the Labour Party. However, in the Swedish case, the power of the central confederation over other unions meant that policy was normally hammered out between the SAP and the LO. This was related to another key feature—the intellectual rigor of many of the proposals and policies, which were as often the creation of the LO as the SAP. Whereas some of the most creative policy proposals in other countries came from figures outside social democracy—for example, John Maynard Keynes—in Sweden they tended to come from the mainstream of the movement. Thus Ernest Wigforss had already devised a countercyclical economic policy so as to stimulate demand and reduce unemployment (anticipating Keynes's General Theory), before becoming minister of finance. Holding this position from 1932 until 1949, he then had the power to implement some of his strategies. Similarly, acceptance of some pioneering ideas in social policy in the 1930s by the eminent social economists Gunnar and Alva Myrdal was facilitated by their position within the social democratic "establishment."

Although the SAP governments did not always proceed as quickly or as radically as some of their supporters hoped, they constantly sought to advance further in relation to the goals of equality and solidarity. Thus at the end of the 1980s, Sweden remained the Western society with the highest percentage of GDP devoted to health, education, and related programs. Moreover, various longitudinal studies in the 1970s and 1980s showed that redistribution continued to be greater in Sweden than in any other country, even though it had the lowest rate of inequality at the beginning of the period of analysis. Some of the significant gains in equality were side effects of other policies. Thus one of the most notable aspects of Swedish social democracy, the progress made in relation to sexual equality, was initially due, to a considerable extent, to the demand for labor in an era of economic expansion. Thus the female participation rate rose from 50% in 1960 to 75% in 1980, the highest in the Organization for Economic Cooperation and Development (OECD), where the average rate was still 50%. In most countries, working women were then confined to the low-paid sector, but because of the general trade union policies of increasing wages in the lowest-paid jobs and of equal pay for

The Swedish economic theorist Gunnar Myrdal (1898–1987) and his wife, Alva (1902–86), seen in this 1970 photograph, coauthored the book *Crisis in the Population Question* (1934). Mr. Myrdal received the Nobel Prize in economics in 1974 for "pioneering work in the theory of money and economic fluctuations and for . . . penetrating analysis of the interdependence of economic, social, and institutional phenomena." Mrs. Myrdal was elected to the Swedish parliament in 1962 and received the Nobel Peace Prize in 1982.

equal work, women gained greater protection than elsewhere. Neither this, nor the rapid expansion of nurseries and childcare centers, necessarily originated either in the commitment to sexual equality or even from social (rather than economic) policy. As will be argued in the next chapter, the relationships between feminism and socialism are complex and involve far more than work-related issues, and in Sweden the role of women's movements was crucial in broadening the conceptions of sexual equality that had originated in the demands of the economy. This relates to a wider point about Swedish social democracy: the way in which it became self-reinforcing as different groups secured a stake in its development.

Tim Tilton has argued that Swedish social democracy has been characterized by five central themes. First, integrative democracy, with democratic decision-making as the ultimate standard of legitimacy. Because the SAP was always committed to creating a society where industrial workers (and later employees as a whole) participated on equal terms in the organization and governance of society, aspects of social and economic democracy were also addressed, but consensual rule remained the strong preference. This was related to the second element, the concept of the "people's home," discussed above, with goals of solidarity and equality of treatment. Third, it was always argued that socioeconomic equality and economic efficiency were complementary rather than contradictory goals, and this was also closely related to the fourth point—the pursuit of a socially controlled market economy, rather than nationalization. During the 1920s, the SAP abandoned the preoccupation with ownership and gradually adopted the notion of shifting the nature of markets through the distribution of income. Over time, this led to an emphasis on bargains with industrialists and active labor market policies, with a gradual paring away of the prerogatives of capitalists through increasing social control.

The fifth theme was the belief that a proper expansion of the public sector extended freedom of choice by enhancing security for ordinary people. This was based on the dual assumptions that the government was democratic and that taxation was not a threat to freedom, but a means of providing public services for the benefit of all. This led to public expenditure mounting to nearly 70% of GNP by 1983, with more than 30% devoted to social services, and marginal taxation rates of 60% for middle-income blue- or white-collar workers and 80% for managers. These rates meant that Sweden's tax revenues accounted for the highest proportion of

Well-run day-care centers for children were developed far earlier in Sweden than in most countries. This one—in Skakholmen, a neighborhood of Stockholm—was photographed in 1975. It subsidized the cost for families who could not afford the full rate.

GDP in any of the OECD countries, and contributed to a backlash from the mid-1980s.

Clearly, these themes constitute a general ideological outlook rather than a rigorous theory, but this shaped a whole gamut of policies. No doubt the same fundamental set of values of equality and solidarity underpinned the stance toward poorer countries, with Sweden consistently devoting one of the highest proportions of GNP to development aid. However, the success of social democracy also depended upon the extent to which its values shifted the nature of the society as a whole. It would have been extremely difficult for the SAP to maintain power for so long—even as the dominant party in a coalition—had its policies been wholly unacceptable to the other parties and to other power holders in society. It is notable that, even when its long period of office was eventually interrupted for the first time in 1976, there was no major break with the system that it had established and, in any case, it soon returned to government. There was therefore good reason to believe that society had now been reconstituted in the image of the SAP. One plausible argument for this proposition rested on the claim that social democracy was in harmony with some pre-existing aspects of Swedish society. Basic literacy was already claimed to be 100% by the seventeenth century and was reinforced by the existence of elementary schools in every village by 1850. This stress on education may have helped to foster a climate of debate and an empirical tradition. More generally, Henry Milner argues that Swedish political culture has been characterized by values rooted in preindustrial society: practical moderation, public spirit, equity, respect for individual autonomy, and a Lutheran attachment to the work ethic. Such values were then reinforced and complemented by social democracy. Certainly, attitudinal surveys appeared to confirm Swedish preeminence in the values of egalitarianism and the desire to resolve conflict through peaceful means.

Yet an emphasis on societal values—as if they are autonomous determinants of behavior—should be treated with some caution. Nor should the long-term climate of tolerance be exaggerated, for there had also been intensive class conflict in the early twentieth century, including a five-month General Strike in 1909. Social attitudes emphasizing solidarity and equality may be fostered by favorable economic and political conditions, but can be eroded if these change. Furthermore, there were always important limits on the extent of equality—set by the parameters of the private ownership system. In any case, the values were not independent but were fostered and reinforced through institutions and organizations.

Sweden has had the highest propensity for people to be involved in organizations of any country in the world. Most important of all, of course, was the fact that in the late 1980s the SAP itself had 1.2 million members (out of a total Swedish population of only 8.4 million). In addition to this, Sweden has also had the highest rate of unionization in the world, the LO was organically linked to the party, and there was also a strong degree of support for it in the other trade union confederations, and in the cooperative movement, which had almost two million

Between August 4 and September 4 of 1909, more than three hundred thousand Swedish workers—backed by their union, the LO (*Landsorganisationen*)—went on a general strike. They were motivated to do so by the actions of the employers' organization, the SAF (*Svenska Arbetsgvarforeningen*), which proposed to cut wages and locked out 80,000 workers in three different industries. This photograph was taken in Stockholm on August 6, 1909, at a rally in support of the striking workers.

members and 90,000 employees. Finally, at their height, the SAP and LO had their own press and educational institutions and wielded considerable influence over a network of non-governmental organizations and popular movements broadly favorable to a social democratic perspective. They were also prodded from the Left, but generally supported, by the small Communist Party (which later became the Left Party). Yet if social democratic values were nurtured by organizations, the success of its project remained dependent upon its ability to strike a bargain with its potential opponents. After all, even at the height of its post-war ascendancy, the SAP only once achieved 50% of the vote (in 1968), more frequently securing 45–50%. It sometimes governed through a coalition (which it dominated) and it always needed the agreement of the business community. What, then, was the economic bargain that underpinned the Swedish model?

The origins of the bargain lay in an agreement in 1938 between the LO and the employers' organization, SAF (*Svenska Arbetsgvarforeningen*), but the system that really reinforced the "model" was based on a report submitted to the LO Congress by its two major economists, Gosta Rehn and Rudolf Meidner, in 1951. Before this, there had been a brief period of wage control and the Rehn-Meidner model was an alternative both to this kind of austerity and to the use of unemployment to control wage levels. It was implemented by the government for the first time during a recession between 1957 and 1959.

The key to the approach was the belief that rising productivity was the essential precondition for increasing wages and financing the development of the welfare state. At the same time, Rehn and Meidner argued, the LO should coordinate wage bargaining so as to give support to the claims of the weakest unions. The originality of the Rehn-Meidner model was that it identified the interests of those in a weak bargaining position with those of the labor movement as a whole. The general principle was of equal pay for equal work (the basis of the "solidaristic" wage policy), which meant that, while some firms faced the possibility of being forced out of business because of the pressure to increase the wages of the lowest paid, wage restraint by the highest-paid workers could lead to the expansion of the most profitable industries. The success of the plan therefore depended upon the supremacy of the LO over its member unions, so that the redistribution could be effected, on active labor market policies (for example, retraining, good information about available opportunities, subsidies for relocation), and general economic expansion. The Rehn-Meidner model also anticipated some possible problems. A commitment to free trade exposed firms experiencing a profit squeeze to international competition so that they could not simply pass on higher wage costs to consumers. At the other end of the scale, the government would use taxation to limit the extent to which the more successful firms could use excessive profits to pay higher wages instead of investing in new capacity. The overall strategy therefore encouraged the concentration of capital, particularly of the large export-oriented firms, and the substitution of capital for labor. By the late 1970s, there was a higher concentration of privately owned resources than in any other Western country. It was on the basis of this successful tripartite bargain between government, unions, and employers that the Swedish welfare state was built. However, the original bargain meant that many of the prerogatives of management had been respected, and that egalitarianism had made little impact on some key aspects of inequality. For example, in the later 1970s, 25% of share capital was held by the top 0.1% of shareholders and 75% by the top 10%. All this would now become relevant as the pace of economic expansion declined and the threats to the Swedish model increased. One episode epitomized a turning point in its fortunes: the crisis over the wage-earner funds proposal.

Pressures and Problems

In the late 1960s the labor movement had become more radical. This was perhaps partly because of the general international climate in the era of "1968," but also as a result of dissatisfaction with some of the practical results of the wage solidarity: the collapse of wage differentials in some sectors, while the most successful manufacturing companies were earning record profits. This led to a series of important reforms, including in industrial democracy. However, in 1976 the LO published the final version of a report on wage-earner funds by Rudolf Meidner. The idea was that legislation should be passed requiring all companies above a certain size to issue new shares corresponding to a proportion of their annual profits. Each year the wage earners would collectively take a share of the equity capital, and the higher the profits the more rapid the transfer would be. At the recommended rate of growth the new funds would control 52% of companies' shares within twenty years.

This was clearly a major step beyond the terms of the previous tripartite bargain and, unusually, the LO had not reached agreement with the SAP before publishing it. In fact the party then played it down in the campaign for the forthcoming general election (which it lost). Subsequently, the party and unions worked together on a series of less radical versions of the project, which was finally implemented in December 1983, following the SAP's return to power in the previous year. However, as soon as the original proposal had been published, the employers mobilized against it in an unprecedented way, including a demonstration of between 75,000 and 100,000 people in Stockholm in October 1981. Supported by a massive press campaign (orchestrated by the employers), this undermined the potential support that there may have been for the original proposal.

Two points are of particular importance. First, it suggested that the LO had gone beyond the employers' understanding of the limits of the bargain that had underpinned the "model." Moves toward greater industrial democracy had been accepted, but the perceived threat to ownership would not be tolerated. Second, the underlying economic and political situation was now beginning to change and, with their new assertiveness, it became less clear that the employers and center and right parties would continue to accept the existing system. By the mid-1980s, the nature of the economy had shifted considerably. With the share of GNP based on exports now at over 30% and Swedish enterprises increasingly multinational, the economy was more exposed to international pressures than thirty years earlier. This was the era of Thatcher and Reagan and the push toward neoliberalism, and with the large exporters, who had always been supported by the government, susceptible to the new international orthodoxies, it was clear that the threats to the Swedish model were growing. Moreover, the SAP and the LO were also suffering from socioeconomic changes that were affecting the labor movement in all advanced industrial countries: the decline in blue-collar work and changing social and political attitudes. All these pressures led to four crucial shifts in Swedish politics.

The first was a decline in the SAP's dominance. Thus in 1991, for the first time since 1932, its share of the vote dropped below 40%, membership having declined by approximately 10% during the 1980s. Moreover, it no longer dominated popular movements, which were now showing the same tendency to focus on single issues (for example, Greenpeace and Amnesty International) as in other countries. Nor was its closeness to the LO so valuable as before, with the decline in blue-collar workers and, by the early 1990s, the percentage of workers' votes going to the SAP was reduced to about 50%. It also discontinued "collective affiliation," loosening the relationship between the party and the labor movement. Second, when in office, the SAP was inevitably influenced by domestic and international pressures. During the 1980s, it certainly resisted the pressures toward the kind of neoliberalism that had been adopted elsewhere, but it did reduce taxation levels and squeezed the public sector, leading to a rise in unemployment and some regressive redistribution of income. There was also privatization of some public sector activities. Third, internationalization of the economy was given impetus by the removal of capital controls in 1989 (having been in place since 1939) and, of still greater importance, by entry into the European Union in 1995. The latter event is of immense significance, not only for the obvious reason that Sweden is now subject to all the legislation and forms of economic integration that make it more difficult to preserve a distinctive system, but also because entry into the EU further fragmented the social democratic consensus. For although it was a social democratic government that initiated the application in 1990, the forces most in favor of membership were large-scale industrialists and their political allies, with the SAP and the LO divided. Some of the strongest opponents of entry were women's groups, who had been closely tied to the SAP and who feared that European integration would result in downward pressure on welfare expenditure. Acceptance of the EU by the SAP leadership thus threatened to further weaken its political support from some of its strongest constituencies. Finally, in 1990, the most specific aspect of the Swedish model—the centralized bargaining system between the SAF and the LO—collapsed. In these circumstances, the kind of tripartite national agreement that had underpinned the Swedish model was no longer possible.

The End of an Era?

All this leaves the question of whether Sweden is still a "social democracy" or whether, through a combination of domestic and international

pressures, it is now converging toward some kind of European advanced capitalist "norm." There is no agreed answer on this. Public expenditure has certainly declined from its peak in 1993 of 70% of GNP to 56.3% in 2002, with social expenditure falling from almost 39% of total GNP in 1993 to 33% in 2002. During the mid-1990s, Sweden also lagged just behind Finland and Denmark as the most equal countries in the world in terms of income distribution. Nor has Sweden been immune to the general xenophobia and racism that has developed in Europe in recent years, undermining some of its claims to solidarity and equality. This was particularly

Sweden entered the European Union in 1995, a move that was largely supported by the leadership of the country's Social Democratic Party (SAP). Despite this, Sweden has not adopted the euro as its official unit of currency, although there are a limited number of places—as shown in this 2008 photograph of a street in Stockholm—where the euro is accepted.

alarming when, in the 1991 election, a newly formed extreme right party, *Ny Demokrati* (New Democracy), achieved 6.7% of the votes and twenty-five seats. This party subsequently disappeared, but in the 2002 election, a mainstream party, the *Folkpartiet* (Liberals), almost tripled its share of the vote from the 1998 election (from 4.7% to 13.3%) by exploiting the immigration issue. While the extreme right had been squeezed out, there were some signs that the values of tolerance had previously been fostered by Sweden's position as a small country with a comparatively homogenous population, and did not necessarily apply so readily to "outsiders."

Despite the changes that have taken place, the fears of many that internationalization and entry into the EU would undermine the whole system do not seem to have been warranted. Trade union membership actually rose in the early 1990s, reaching a record level of 86% of all employees (subsequently declining to 83% in 2003). Women have retained their prominent role in social life; 50% of those in the 1994–98 cabinet were women, and although this was reduced slightly after the election in 2002 (to ten out of twenty-two), the proportion of women in parliament rose to its highest ever level, at 45%. This strengthened support for high social expenditure, to which women have been particularly committed. While the welfare consensus may not have been so strong as earlier, and while elements of privatization had been introduced, there was still a very widespread belief in economic success as the basis for welfare rather than acceptance of neoliberal ideology. Both total government and social expenditure have certainly fallen as a percentage of GNP, but they remain the highest in the world, with the lowest level of child poverty at 2.6% (compared, for example, to 7.9% in France, 19.8% in the UK, and 22.4% in the U.S.). It may therefore be the case that the values, institutions, and relationships that had been fostered over generations will prove sufficiently resilient to withstand some of the pressures, even if adaptations are necessary.

The overall conclusion from the Swedish case is that, in certain circumstances, and within certain limitations, a well-organized and imaginative social democratic movement was able to make significant progress toward the goals of equality and solidarity for the benefit of ordinary people. It is much less clear whether such a strategy could succeed to the same extent now, but Sweden's earlier achievements, and the support for social democratic values that were thus nurtured, provide it with significant advantages in withstanding international neoliberal pressures.

Cuban Communism

The Revolution

Fidel Castro (1927–) assumed control of Cuban politics after a successful revolution in January 1959, and from the early 1960s a communist regime was progressively established. The typical single-party/state system was created, and the country became closely aligned with the Soviet Union, with increasing economic dependence upon it after 1970. However, if Cuba became communist, this was not the case in 1959 and many characteristics of the regime were shaped by the nature of the initial revolution.

Ever since gaining independence from Spain in 1895, Cuban life had been marked by its economic dependency upon sugar, frequent military coups to prevent radical change, and U.S. domination. From the 1930s, Cuban governments had depended upon military support in the figure of Fulgencio Batista, and in 1940 he won the presidential election himself and ruled for four years. Subsequently, his influence appeared to wane, but in 1952, when he failed to win a further presidential election, he resorted to a coup d'état, which was supported by Washington. Although he called elections in 1954, it was clear that he had no intention of abandoning power and, as the sole candidate, he was reelected for a four-year term in 1955. The Batista regime was corrupt and repressive, and Cuba was a highly unequal society, with

Fulgencio Batista (1901–73) held the rank of sergeant in the Cuban army when he took over the reins of power in a 1933 military action known as the Revolt of the Sergeants. He went on to become Cuba's president (1940–44); after another coup in 1952, he became Cuba's leader again—until U.S. support for his regime was finally withdrawn in 1958. This November 10, 1938, photograph shows Batista waving to the crowds upon his arrival in Washington, D.C., for an official visit—his first trip outside Cuba in thirty-seven years.

extreme poverty in many parts of the island. Support for revolution grew during the second half of the 1950s, as even many liberals came to believe that Batista would not yield power through negotiation. By late 1958, it was also evident that Castro and his guerrilla army would be the dominant force in the revolution.

In 1952, Castro, as a twenty-five-year-old law graduate, had been appalled by Batista's coup and on July 26, 1953, he and his closest followers had attempted to start a revolution by taking control of a military barracks. This was a total failure, and he was imprisoned, but then released in a general amnesty two years later. After concluding that only insurrection would dislodge the regime, he and his closest associates went into exile, returning in December 1956. Over the next two years, his July 26th movement (named after the date of the abortive insurrection in 1953) simultaneously built alliances with other groups (including liberal politicians) and engaged in violent conflicts with the army. By late 1958, the Batista regime was finding it impossible to govern and the U.S. withdrew its support, hoping that it would be able to reach agreement with the revolutionary forces. It was in these circumstances that Batista fled, and Castro, the rebel army, and the July 26th movement assumed control. There was no doubt that the revolution was popular, but it was not yet clear what it implied.

The most explicit aspects of the movement's statements were the total repudiation of the past, the determination to renovate Cuban politics, the rejection of foreign intervention, and the demand that the rebel army would be the sole guarantor of a new Cuba. Nor was the initial program of the revolutionary government explicitly socialist. Its main feature was agrarian reform and it also introduced progressive tax policies, which favored Cuban over foreign investments, non-sugar over sugar sectors, small over large business, and the provinces over Havana. Rents were reduced and there were also taxes on exports and the introduction of foreign exchange controls. However, the apparently limited nature of the revolution was deceptive for two reasons: first, because of its social significance, and second, because of the centralization of power by Castro and his closest comrades.

In the late 1950s, Cuba was ranked among the top five countries in Latin America on a range of indicators, but over 40% of the rural population was illiterate, fewer than 10% of rural homes had electricity, and fewer than 3% of rural households had indoor plumbing. There was widespread malnutrition, and there were only three general hospitals in the countryside, with medical facilities concentrated in Havana. The revolutionary regime was the first one that had ever unambiguously concentrated on the poor and ordinary people rather than the dominant economic interests. The land redistribution and the improvement of conditions on the large farms taken over by the government had an immediate impact, and the rent reductions transferred approximately 15% of national income from property owners to wage workers and peasants. Large landowners and mill owners had generally opposed the revolution from the start, but many industrialists had supported it. However, Castro frightened them as early as February 1959 with a statement attributing all blame for the current economic situation to the system of private enterprise, immoral governments, and the wealthy. Subsequently, the government's mediation in disputes between workers and employers overwhelmingly favored the former. Support for the revolution among the dominant classes quickly waned, while the enthusiasm of ordinary people was growing. At the same time, Castro strengthened his grip on power.

While liberals and reformist nationalists were included in the first government, it was clear that Castro and the rebel army were in charge. Castro became prime minister in the middle of February 1959 and soon isolated his opponents. Revolutionary tribunals also judged and then executed some 500 members of Batista's police and security agents, and fears that this would continue led many of the propertied classes and nonrevolutionary politicians into exile. However, Castro also ensured that the Moscow-backed Popular Socialist Party (PSP)

Revolutionary leader Fidel Castro (1926–) waves to a cheering crowd upon his arrival in Havana, Cuba, in 1959. Despite intense American pressure, Castro would remain in power long after the downfall of the Soviet bloc.

was kept under control. The PSP had originally been opposed to Castro's July 26th movement, regarding it as "adventurist," but had ultimately come to believe that revolution was necessary and a section had joined the rebel army in summer 1958. The PSP had considerable experience in trade unionism, and Castro waited until the July 26th movement had secured an overwhelming majority in the unions before using his influence to unite the two organizations in the Trade Union Confederation (CTC). His aim was no doubt to prevent the establishment of rival centers of power, but then also to use relevant organizations to promote his priorities. This determination to secure full control was equally evident in his attitude to the political process.

Almost immediately after the revolution, the dominant economic classes and the U.S. called for elections. But in May 1959, Castro made it clear that the first priorities were to promote employment, expand healthcare, extend education, and create a new political consciousness. A year later he told a million Cubans in Havana that the government would not hold elections. Given the history of corruption and manipulation that had characterized the island's politics, this was not viewed as a problem and the response from the crowd was that the people had already voted for Fidel. The new regime thus initially rested on charismatic authority and the popularity of the reforms, rather than the institutional structures of Soviet-style communism. In the spring and summer of 1959 Castro had even claimed that the revolution was humanist rather than socialist in character. However, there was a final key factor that would shape the regime: its relationships with the U.S. and the Soviet Union.

The 1902 Platt amendment, which allowed the U.S. to intervene in Cuban affairs whenever order was threatened, had been formally abrogated by Roosevelt in 1934, but its spirit lived on. The U.S. government had been lukewarm about Castro from the start, and his visit to Washington in April 1959 had done nothing to allay its anxiety. The Administration had probably expected him to ask for aid and might have responded positively to such a request on conditions that would have bound the new government to the U.S. Castro failed to ask, and the CIA and State Department almost immediately began to plan his overthrow, with the rhetoric of confrontation escalating on both sides. In February 1960, a high-level Soviet delegation visited Cuba and signed its first favorable trade deal, followed by the establishment of full diplomatic relations. U.S. action against the regime then increased, culminating in an abortive attempt to overthrow it by supporting the so-called Bay of Pigs invasion by Cuban exiles in April 1961. The U.S. also initiated an economic embargo against the island. All this both strengthened popular enthusiasm for the revolution and fundamentally affected its nature. The previous September, when U.S. intervention appeared imminent, Castro had created the Committees for the Defense of the Revolution (CDR), and these units of volunteers played a key role in defeating the counter-revolutionary attempt. Popular enthusiasm for the defense of national independence now combined with the socioeconomic appeal of the revolution to create a still closer bond between Castro and the masses. However, he also strengthened his alliances to ensure that U.S. pressure could be resisted. The pro-Soviet PSP became a more important partner in the governing coalition, and the relationship with Moscow was cemented, leading to the installation of nuclear missiles against the U.S. and near world war in October 1962.

It was only in April 1961, on the eve of the Bay of Pigs invasion, that Castro declared that the revolution was socialist, and subsequently Cuba began to evolve toward a political system that resembled that of the Soviet bloc. In that year, the July 26th movement, the PSP, and various other groupings formed the Integrated Revolutionary Organization—an embryonic single party. However, Castro was in no hurry to take the next step and waited until 1965 for the formal establishment of the Communist Party. Whether he always intended this kind of evolution or whether the dynamics of the domestic and international situation led to communism remains controversial. But in either case, it is clear that the origins and early development of the revolution continued to lend it very specific characteristics. Cuba was never a Soviet satellite in the same way as the states in East-Central Europe—both history and geography were decisive in this respect.

Advances and Setbacks

The social objectives of the new regime were immediately evident as thousands of young volunteers were sent to rural areas to spread literacy and simultaneously to learn about agriculture in the hope that this would break down the divisions between town and country. Hundreds of new schools were built, with teacher training massively increased. Healthcare was also taken to rural areas, with the building of rural clinics. However, there were economic difficulties, with a drop in sugar yields of over 30% between 1959 and 1963. This soon led to more rapid socialization, and between 1964 and 1970 the whole of industry, commerce, and finance were nationalized and 70% of agriculture was taken over by the state. There were also wage increases for the poorest-paid workers and moves toward an equalization of earnings and consumption. However, the most radical phase of the revolution, from the middle of the decade, was the attempt to dispense with market incentives completely.

Ernesto "Che" Guevara (1928–67), one of Castro's closest associates before 1959, was the most sophisticated theorist in the revolution, with a particular interest in the humanism in Marx's early writings. During the first half of the 1960s, while holding a succession of key economic posts, he disputed conventional communist ideas about the necessity for material incentives in the initial construction of a socialist

The Argentinian-born revolutionary Che Guevara (1928–67) led an attack on Santa Clara, Cuba, in late 1958 that gave Fidel Castro the deciding victory in his takeover of power from Fulgencio Batista. This photograph of Che in his familiar military fatigues was taken after the battle, on January 1, 1959.

economy. In addition to central planning, his emphasis was on urging the population to work for moral rather than material incentives, with city workers also volunteering to assist on the sugar harvest for the sake of society as a whole. All kinds of nonmonetary incentives (such as flags, diplomas, and titles) were awarded both individually and collectively to those who worked overtime or showed exceptional productivity. This was made more palatable by a simultaneous expansion of free social services, with the whole of education, medical care, social security, day-care, and much housing free of charge. Nevertheless, it was asking a lot to expect those who were already working extremely hard to do still more without any material rewards, and until 1966 some attention was also paid to conventional communists and Soviet advisers. Following Marx's own position in the *Critique of the Gotha Program* (see Chapter 1), they argued that, with a low level of development, workers could not be expected to respond to appeals to sacrifice themselves for the good of society and therefore needed higher wages and bonuses for increased productivity. However, Castro endorsed Guevara's approach in 1966, culminating in the revolutionary offensive of 1968–70, in which the whole economic strategy was focused on the aim of harvesting and pro-cessing 10 million tons of sugar in 1970. The stress was on exhortation, but there were also some rather threatening aspects of social control: for example, in 1969 an identity card system was introduced listing a worker's merits and demerits. In the event, the target was not reached: only 8.5 million tons of sugar were harvested (compared with approxi-mately 6 million in 1959) and production in other key sectors declined, probably because of the preoccupation with sugar.

In reality, the moral approach may have been based on some cogent economic considerations rather than pure ideology: above all, that it was much cheaper to persuade people to work in a "push for communism" than to pay them to do so. Whether or not this was so, the reasons for the failure are interesting. Some of the explanation related to external factors—low world sugar prices and reductions in Soviet aid because of opposition to Cuban revolutionary zeal. However, it was also for domestic reasons, including resentments at increased work without material incentives. This led to foot-dragging, absenteeism, black-market activity, and other forms of quiet resistance through which the Cuban population found covert ways to defy unpopular policies.

The 1970 sugar crisis led to a complete reorientation in policy, with more reference to Soviet experience, formalized in Cuban adherence to the Soviet economic bloc (Comecon) in 1972. In 1973 the Trade Union Confederation, which was heavily controlled by the Communist Party, but nevertheless sensitive to the popular mood, argued in favor of more material incentives and the government shifted in this direction and also increased the production of consumer goods. The post-1970 reforms also led to a less egalitarian pay structure and some market-related reforms, with greater decentralization and more autonomy and profit incentives for individual units in the state sector in both industry and agriculture. There was also more tolerance for limited private economic activity, although this was coupled with incentives to form farming cooperatives, which increased very rapidly in this period. Many more goods were also made available without rationing, although basic goods were still distributed in this way so as to protect the poor. These changes strengthened support for the regime in both rural and urban areas and, despite an economic downturn in 1976, the average annual growth rate between 1981 and 1983 was 7% at a time when it was negative in Latin America as a whole.

It was when the annual growth rate was almost 14% between 1971 and 1975 that a major effort was made to increase female participation in the workforce, suggesting (as in Sweden) that economic pressures were important in initiating measures to bring about greater gender equality. The participation of women had increased only slightly from the Batista era (from 13% in 1956 to 18% in 1970), although there had already been a major change in the nature of women's employment. From 1974 a range of gender equality measures were introduced and by the mid-1980s female participation had climbed to 37%. This was the highest level of formal sector employment for women in the whole of Latin America and was consolidated by the increasing proportion of women in higher education, rising to over 55% of all enrollments by 1986–87. However, women still suffered disproportionately from unemployment when there was a downturn in the economy in 1976, and they were still excluded from several jobs.

Taken as a whole, the period between 1970 and 1985 was probably the most successful economically, socially, and politically for the regime. Nevertheless, there were also underlying problems. First, the drop in the growth rate in 1976 had been partially offset by Soviet subsidies—particularly the purchase of guaranteed quantities of sugar above world prices. However, this reinforced Cuban dependency on both sugar and Soviet and Comecon support. Second, at the time of rapid growth, Castro had also sought greater Western trade, tourism, foreign investment, and borrowing, but some of this had perverse effects. The regime was left with debts to the West that were difficult to repay and, while tourism brought foreign currency, it also stimulated discontent by exposing the population to other influences. Thus in 1980, 125,000 people were allowed to leave the island, partly because their dissatisfaction had been exacerbated by tales of the good life elsewhere. The changes of direction had also led to problems within the political leadership, with eleven ministers dropped in the same year.

None of this was catastrophic for the regime, but in 1986 there was a further change of direction—albeit of a contradictory kind. The government proclaimed that it was necessary to rectify errors and negative tendencies that had developed. Castro argued that too much capitalism had been embraced and the memory of Che Guevara was invoked to renew an emphasis on moral values. On the surface, this appeared to be a return to the first phase of the revolution. Thus there was a clampdown on many elements of the market in favor of enhanced state control of the economy. However, the government simultaneously pursued Western economic ties far more aggressively, providing incentives and establishing semiautonomous state agencies specifically for joint ventures with Western capital, and tourism increased very rapidly. A drop in the sugar price and a reduction by 50% of the other major form of Soviet subsidy (a concession which enabled Cuba to re-export Soviet oil for hard currency), led to a debt of nearly $5 billion in 1986. At the same time, and largely because of these difficulties, dependency on Comecon became greater than ever—accounting for 86% of Cuba's total trade in 1986. The government no doubt hoped that increased austerity and state control domestically, coupled with an attempt to open up externally, would reduce deficits and increase the stock of hard currency. It failed to do so and the economic stringency also created political problems.

While constantly invoking revolutionary ideology, Castro was now actually undermining some of the advances in labor conditions that had been made earlier, and there was also an increase in prices, a drop of living standards, and a slight fall in wages. Such changes, coupled with the restrictions on the market sector, again led to resentments and a covert undermining of state policies. At the same time, some officials in the sectors dealing with Western capitalism took advantage of their privileged access to foreign exchange for personal gain and built up informal power networks. In 1989, this led to the public execution of four very senior officials, with others imprisoned or dismissed from office. The trials were televised, no doubt to intimidate others.

Crisis: The Collapse of the Soviet Bloc

By the late 1980s, the Cuban economy was in an acutely vulnerable position: near total dependency on the Soviet bloc, excessive reliance on sugar, indebtedness to the capitalist world, and few competitive products with high-income yields. The collapse of communism in Eastern Europe in 1989 and the subsequent disintegration of the Soviet Union were then crippling blows, and the Cubans assessed the cost to their economy at $5.7

Terrible shortages plagued Cuba in the 1990s after the collapse of the Soviet bloc. The people in this photograph—taken some time between 1991 and 1994—stood in line for food next to posters of some of the military heroes credited with repelling U.S. troops during the Bay of Pigs (Playa Girón) invasion in 1961. Che Guevara was director of instruction for the Cuban armed forces during the invasion.

billion in 1992, with the loss of 70% of their purchasing power. Perhaps no modern economy suffered a comparable collapse in the twentieth century except in conditions of war. The U.S. clearly believed that additional pressure would bring about the end of the regime, and in 1992 passed the Cuba Democracy Act, which tightened the embargo and specified that only the total removal of the Communist Party from power would be acceptable, and this was reinforced by further legislation in 1996.

The impact of such economic and political pressures on any state would be immense. In effect, Cuba was turned into a siege economy with power shut off every day in each neighborhood, shortages of necessities, and queues for rationed food. The need for people to spend so much time dealing with the basic requirements of life inevitably also led to a decline in productivity, although many factories could not function in any case, because they lacked the raw materials or spare parts. In these circumstances, the Castro regime attempted to maintain an equality of misery, with the continuation of free medicine and education, but doctors needed to spend much of their time searching for equipment or drugs, and schools were also short of the basic requirements. University admissions were reduced and a greater emphasis was placed on more practical education. This was related to a new attempt to create self-sufficiency in food production, with the creation of agricultural brigades. However, the government was aware that neither the economy nor the social system could survive simply on the basis of collective austerity and sacrifice, and it simultaneously pursued a more aggressive attempt to attract foreign investment, with elements of privatization. Above all, this involved a bid to turn Cuba into a major tourist center. While this certainly brought some economic benefits, it also had some highly negative effects.

Almost immediately after the attainment of power in 1959, Castro had ended the sleazy nightclub culture which the island had built up during its dependency on the USA. Some of this was now restored and sex tourism resumed. The influx of tourists also had marked economic effects. For some time an informal dollar economy had been developing, but in 1993 this was legalized in an attempt to gain as much hard currency as possible. Over the next decade, this led to a situation in which the dollar economy became increasingly dominant, while poorer people were reliant on the rationing system. Similar two-tier systems grew up elsewhere. Foreign tourists were given privileges of various kinds (including fuel allocations), while many Cubans were still struggling with acute shortages. Likewise, those who worked in the tourist industry received bonuses and tips, while those outside it had few such opportunities. Although the economy began to grow again after 1994, its nature had now changed, and both the renewed poverty and the impact of tourism inevitably exacerbated the political problems.

Increasing pressure from Washington, particularly with George W. Bush in the White House, reinforced the difficulties, while Castro's periodic reliance on overt repression strengthened the hand of the Cuban lobby in Florida in ensuring that no concessions were made. In this context, the imprisonment of seventy-five dissidents and the execution of three people for hijacking a ship and trying to sail it to Florida in April 2003 suggested that the regime was fighting for survival rather than progressively moving toward the professed goals of the revolution. Apart from the support of the Chavez government in Venezuela, Cuba was soon almost entirely isolated, with the EU also hardening its line. Yet the regime's endurance was remarkable, and two years later the prognosis was uncertain. On the one hand, the U.S. stranglehold was constantly tightened, with restrictions on dollar remittances, obstacles imposed on U.S. food sales to Cuba, and tougher curbs on commerce, visas, and travel. On the other hand, Cuban biotech and medical exports increased, the discovery of oil in the Gulf of Mexico provided a new lifeline, ties with several Latin American countries were strengthened, and the EU edged toward the resumption of normal diplomatic relations. In October 2004 Castro had even retaliated against the U.S. by announcing that American currency would no longer be accepted in Cuba and imposing a 10% commission on the use of dollars. Serious problems remained, but the Cuban leader exuded confidence during a five-hour speech on state television in March 2005.

Evaluating Castro's Regime

In 1959, the Cuban revolution had based itself on the aspirations of the masses, and during the early years of the new regime its aims were demonstrably socialist: the elimination of poverty, and the construction of a new egalitarian society based on cooperation and social solidarity. All this was to be carried out on the doorstep of a bitterly hostile superpower that would use all available means to subvert and overthrow Castro's state. How should the record of postrevolutionary Cuba be evaluated?

By any standards, the social achievements of the Cuban regime were impressive in relation to the goals of reducing poverty and creating equality. The medical advances were particularly remarkable, with Cuba soon having the most doctors, nurses, and hospital beds per capita in Latin America—an achievement even more remarkable in view of the fact that about 50% of the country's doctors went into exile soon after the revolution. A special feature of Cuban medical development was its attempt to equalize provision between the towns and the countryside. Cuba thus became the only Latin American nation with a universal system of free healthcare across the country, and the diversity of provision was also exceptional. This was reflected in life expectation, which improved from being the third highest in the region (at 59) before the revolution to the highest (at 76) in 1992, and also in infant mortality rates, so that in 1990 the death rate for children in Havana was about half that for Washington, D.C. Moreover, the quality and quantity of healthcare in the U.S. was far more discriminatory in terms of both class and race than in Cuba. The achievements in education were equally remarkable, with free primary, secondary, technical, and higher education for all, and a literacy rate of 96.4% by the 1990s. There were also major gains in relation to race inequality. Before the revolution, black Cubans had been excluded from many public facilities, but such discrimination was outlawed at the beginning of the new regime. Equal access to education meant that there was a significant improvement in the number of Afro-Cubans achieving high positions in Cuban society, even though it still appears that black Cubans are overrepresented in the lower echelons of the labor market. As already noted, the role of women changed fundamentally in Cuban society, with a dramatic improvement in their social, economic, and political position. This also led to a decline in birth and fertility rates, with Cuba's pattern of family size and demography far closer to the typical advanced industrial society than to its Latin American neighbors.

The regime attempted to maintain its social achievements after the fall of the Soviet bloc, but inevitably the economic collapse made it extremely difficult to do so. Sustainable socialism needs to be established on the basis of a sustainable economy. However, it also needs to be built on strong political support, and in this respect the record is mixed.

The revolutionary regime certainly sought to establish social solidarity and cooperation and, in many respects, it succeeded in doing so—particularly in the early stages. There is no doubt that such institutions as the CDR were constructed on the basis of genuine enthusiasm to defend the new regime—particularly against the threat of U.S. intervention. There were also frequent manifestations of social solidarity; for example, in the campaigns for urban workers to help in the countryside. No doubt, the success of such events always rested on an element of social control and propaganda, but they still had considerable significance in demonstrating the bonds across society and between society and government. Nevertheless, mass mobilization of this kind is not in itself democratic and this raises the issue of political institutions.

During the 1960s the Communist Party and the CDR were used as dual governing organs and, at their peak, they had up to three million members (out of a population of eleven million). But the party itself maintained power in comparatively few hands and did not even hold its first congress until 1975. After the failure of the 1970 sugar campaign, the limitations of the CDR were recognized, and in 1976 popular participation in policy implementation was channeled through new organizations called People's Power, which had a role in supervising government agencies, and formulating laws and regulations for society as a whole. However, such attempts to create a form of civil society were always limited by the influence of reliable party members in the institutions of People's Power and the Trade Union Confederation. Moreover, the highest echelons of the party always took the decisions at governmental level, although it was never formally an institution of government. No factions were allowed in the party and, although there was theoretically a right to strike, this was never used. Some of the intermediate institutions, particularly the CDR, the Trade Union Confederation (CTC), and the Cuban Women's Federation (FMC), provided a useful sounding board for the leadership, and complaints sometimes led to changes in policy. However, these were not organizations through which real opposition could develop, and those who sought to challenge the communist system, or existing policies, would normally be jailed.

After the collapse of the Soviet bloc, some effort was made to introduce limited reforms into the political system. In 1991, the party payroll was greatly reduced and more direct elections were introduced, reducing the ability of senior echelons simply to choose committee members. There was also an attempt to involve the population as a whole by enabling people to put forward their complaints before the Party Congress that year. Three million did so, with over a million opinions voiced on a whole range of topics, possibly with some impact on educational policy. However, the elections of 1993 and 1998 were more like plebiscites than choices of government policy, and Castro's dominance was not affected by the institutional reforms.

This lack of robust pluralist institutions, coupled with the existence of social solidarity and cooperation, raises two questions about the Cuban experience. The first is empirical: will the solidarity, which was constructed partly through Castro's own charismatic authority, be sufficient to withstand the pressures on the regime after his death? Many analysts are rather pessimistic about this. For example, Susan Eckstein has stressed the way in which the existing intermediate organizations have been used as transmission belts for new governmental policies, thereby undermining their current ability to defend the gains of the revolution. This could mean that, in the event of the collapse of the regime, there would be no nongovernmental organizations to

Raúl Castro (1931–), president of the Cuban Council of State and commander-in-chief of the Cuban armed forces, arrives at the Bolivarian Alternative of the Americas (ALBA) summit at the Contemporary Arts Museum in Cumana, Venezuela, on April 16, 2009.

defend the social gains achieved since 1959 against a Washington-led neoliberal assault. However, others emphasize the extent to which the revolution is embedded in the popular consciousness and imply that it still has the potential for renewal in a post-Castro regime. But whatever the future holds, there is a second, and more theoretical, issue concerning the nature of socialism itself.

The Cuban regime has apparently believed that democracy is inherent within the social achievements. Raúl Castro, the brother and heir apparent of Fidel, made this quite clear in August 1974:

> Even without representative institutions, our revolutionary state is
> and always was democratic. A state like ours, which represents the

interest of the working class, no matter what its form and structure, is more democratic than any other state in history.

However, most noncommunist traditions of socialism would not accept that the goal of social equality is a substitute for that of political equality (even though they might agree that it is a precondition for it). From this perspective, Cuban socialism would be defective in the crucial sphere of democracy even if it managed to survive through mass mobilization and social solidarity. Moreover, in the long run, this may not be solely a matter of theory or of principle, but also of practical politics. For people may need to believe that they are able to voice dissent and seek to influence outcomes through independent institutions. If so, this would suggest that sustainable socialism depends upon active support and political freedoms.

Sweden, Cuba, and Socialism

Both Sweden and Cuba have achieved much in relation to the socialist goals of equality, cooperation, and social solidarity. Clearly, their systems differed very markedly and the two countries were also at very different stages of development when such goals were introduced. Yet the two case studies have revealed some similarities. First, it is evident that in both cases the social achievements remained dependent on sustainable economic success and became far more difficult to uphold when growth faltered. Furthermore, as time went on, it was also clear that the domestic economies could not be isolated from international economic pressures. Second, while egalitarianism was normally welcomed by poorer sections of the community, in neither state was it universally popular. Thus when the Cuban regime attempted to build the revolution without material rewards in the 1960s, the reaction against this led to greater incentives and inequality of pay in the next period. Similarly, the egalitarianism of the solidarity wages system and high taxation in Sweden led to a backlash in the 1970s and 1980s. This suggests that equality goals can never be taken for granted by either communist or social democratic governments. Third, both the Swedish and Cuban models have passed their peak. In the Cuban case, the regime was fighting for survival as soon as the Soviet collapse occurred and one of the results of this was the introduction of more elements of capitalism, particularly through tourism. In Sweden too the industrial relations bargaining system that had underpinned its social model had been eroded and elements of privatization had been introduced into public services. This was part of a wider phenomenon that will be examined in Chapter 4.

There are also important contrasts between the Cuban and Swedish experiences. Castro's revolution transformed Cuban society to a far greater extent than any impact made by social democracy on Sweden, where the system of private ownership remained in a very concentrated form, and the changes that took place were always dependent upon compromises with political opponents. However, while the transformation in Cuba certainly elicited popular support, it was constructed from above through state- and party-dominated institutions. In Sweden the independent civil society organizations ready to defend the social model proved to be quite robust. One of the principal reasons why neo-liberal pressures had made much less impact on the welfare system in Sweden by the early twenty-first century than many people had feared fifteen years earlier was the determination of trade unions and women's movements to prevent this. While the Swedish

economy had not suffered the kind of devastation faced by Cuba—
and its political system was therefore not tested in the same way—the
resilience of its civil society was notable.

It is also instructive to consider the experiences of Sweden and Cuba
in the context of the two traditions they represented. Both states, it will
be recalled, were chosen not because they were typical exemplars, but
because they demonstrated the potential, as well as the limitations, of their
respective traditions. Swedish social democracy may have coexisted with
capitalism, rather than creating the kind of socialism originally envisaged
in the nineteenth century, but it created a relatively egalitarian and cooperative society through democratic means. Built on an unusual degree
of social consensus, the model that was created has been trimmed but is
still recognizable. Outside Scandinavia, social democracy has not shown
the same resilience because it never succeeded in constructing a society
in its own image. In such countries as Britain, France, and Germany,
social democratic parties normally formed governments only sporadically
and were not granted much opportunity to leave a lasting imprint on the
social fabric. But nor were they always very clear about the kind of society
they were trying to build. All this made it easier for neoliberalism to
undermine the postwar consensus on social welfare and full employment
after the mid-1970s, particularly in Britain.

The experience of Cuba in relation to that of other communist
regimes is still more telling. The rapid collapse of the Soviet bloc in
Eastern Europe in 1989—once it became clear that Mikhail Gorbachev
(1931–), the Soviet leader, would not use military means to sustain the
states there—indicated the erosion of popular support for the existing
systems. The causes of the disintegration of the Soviet Union itself two
years later were highly complex, but also suggested that, even after

more than seventy years in power, the communist state had not secured sufficient legitimacy to withstand the pressures to which it was now subjected. While the single-party political system of China may have remained intact, it has embraced capitalist economics, the market, and inequality, and Vietnam has moved in a similar direction. North Korea has changed to a lesser degree, but it remains a hermetically sealed militarist dictatorship. Cuba is therefore alone in maintaining fundamental elements of its social and economic system against sustained U.S. pressure. It remains to be seen whether a post-Castro regime will demonstrate the same resilience or whether the revolutionary state has always been constructed around the personality of its founder.

THREE

New Left—Enrichment and Fragmentation

●

DURING THE THIRD QUARTER of the twentieth century, there was a gradual erosion of the dominance of communism and social democracy over concepts of socialism, leading to the emergence of a "New Left": 1956 is often taken as the pivotal date in this process. In the case of communism, the reasons are quite evident: after having denounced Stalin's brutal repression at the Soviet Party Congress in February, Nikita Krushchev, the Soviet leader, initiated an invasion of Hungary in November in order to ensure its continued adherence to the Soviet-dominated bloc. These two events led to an unprecedented exodus of Communist Party

The year 1968 was a watershed for leftist movements worldwide. It was a time of pro-labor, pro-socialist protests and demonstrations, many of which were led by students. This photograph, taken in May of 1968, shows a group of students displaying their solidarity with workers occupying the Renault plant at Boulogne-Billancourt, France, on the outskirts of Paris.

members, particularly in Western Europe, and gradually undermined Moscow's control of world communism. This was reinforced by the sharp deterioration in relations between the Soviet Union and China leading, during the 1960s, to "Maoism" mounting a challenge to communist orthodoxy. In the case of social democracy, there was no similar cataclysm, because there was no equivalent center, and each national party followed its own trajectory. In fact, it may be argued that the real crisis for social democracy arose much later with the stalled growth and increasing impact of economic internationalization from the 1970s, and this will be discussed in the next chapter.

However, the crisis of communism was also bound to affect social democracy, for Moscow had been the center of Marxist thought since 1917 and the cold war had reinforced this tendency. Dissident ex-communists now encouraged a renewed interest in Marxism from those on the left who had never wanted to associate themselves with the Soviet Union. Others who rejected social democracy as too timid were drawn to new forms of extra-parliamentary politics that challenged existing theories and practices across a whole range of activity. The emergence of this New Left culminated in another historical "moment": 1968, when student-led movements unleashed protests against established authority across much of the world, most notably in France.

The New Left was never a coherent movement, but was rather a shorthand for a whole range of ideas and tendencies that fell outside the dominant traditions. A shared assumption of both communists and social democrats had been the primacy of the organized working class and this was now called into question in both theory and practice. Marxists thinkers, who rejected the orthodox emphasis on economics, also became influential in the New Left. In particular, the Frankfurt School, which

The philosopher Herbert
Marcuse (1898–1979), sometimes
called the Father of the New Left,
taught philosophy and politics at
Brandeis University from 1958
to 1965. Among his students
there were the American political
activists Abbie Hoffman and
Angela Davis. This photograph of
Marcuse was taken in 1968, when
he was a professor at the University
of California at San Diego.

had always emphasized the importance of consciousness rather than class
as the source of social transformation, was rediscovered, and Herbert Marcuse (1898–1979) became particularly important. In *Eros and Civilization*
(1955) he drew on Marx and Freud to argue in favor of both social and
sexual liberation, while in *One-Dimensional Man* (1964) he argued that
the working class had become entirely integrated into advanced industrial
society. Revolutionary transformation would now depend on "outsiders,"
including ethnic minorities and radical intellectuals. Although his work
was often obscure, its "message" was in harmony with the movements of
1968. Battling against existing power structures and sexual conventions,

students could cite Marcuse to legitimize their aspirations to create a new world. Another earlier figure whose work now became widely appreciated was Antonio Gramsci (1891–1937), the Italian communist leader who had been imprisoned by Mussolini from 1926 until his death. In his prison writings, he dealt extensively with the extent to which capitalist domination (hegemony), particularly in Western Europe, rested on ideological factors, rather than overt aspects of power. He stressed the need for socialists to be able to create a counter-hegemonic project— a new "common sense," based on alternative ideas and cultural constructs. This emphasis, which had some similarities with that of such thinkers as Stuart Hall (1932–) and Raymond Williams (1921–1988), led many on the New Left to broaden the definition of the "political" by including the realm of culture in its widest sense. Far more attention was now also paid to aspects of Marx that had generally been ignored by both the Second and Third Internationals—particularly to some of his earlier writing, in which "humanist" and philosophical considerations had appeared to predominate over political economy. His concept of "alienation," which brought together the realms of consciousness and economic exploitation, again appeared particularly relevant in the era of revolt in 1968.

Yet the New Left was not always deeply theoretical or even specifically socialist. For example, the Campaign for Nuclear Disarmament was the biggest mass movement in Britain in the late 1950s and early 1960s and was supported by the New Left, but it was fueled far more by moral outrage than any conventional socialist notions. More generally, there was also a whole range of direct action movements in the latter 1960s and 1970s, including squatters' movements, tenants' cooperatives, and women's groups. Some of these included people with a coherent socialist doctrine, some based themselves on anarchist ideas, but there were also numerous activists who were drawn to radical politics on particular issues without regarding themselves as socialist. International developments also fueled the protests. The biggest single issue was opposition to the American-led war against the North Vietnamese, which generated major campaigns and demonstrations in many parts of the world. But when, in August 1968, the Soviet Union and some of its allies invaded Czechoslovakia to crush an attempt to establish a more pluralist form of communism there, the gulf between much of the New Left and pro-Soviet communists was further widened.

On the other hand, many of the protesters who were socialist were not really "New Left." For this was the era in which communist parties were now also challenged by groups that claimed revolutionary Marxist credentials. In particular, there was a plethora of small parties which argued that, in one way or another, the Soviet Union had betrayed the revolution but that socialism could still be established by a vanguard party following the "correct" line. Many of these were inspired by Leon Trotsky, who had argued that the rot had set in once Stalin had abandoned the goal of permanent revolution and had attempted to introduce socialism in a single country. Others looked to Mao, emphasizing the revolutionary potential of the masses and need for vigilance against Soviet "revisionism." These Trotskyist and Maoist parties added to the diversity, and they played an active role in many of the campaigns and protest movements of the era.

By the 1970s, the New Left had generated new social movements, which maintained that the dominant forms of socialist theory and practice had been inadequate because they had marginalized or ignored the issues that were now being raised, and they argued that socialism could be enriched by broadening its range. However, the defenders of orthodoxy feared that the whole socialist project would be undermined by excessive concentration on these issues, leading to fragmentation. No doubt both were right, and certainly it now became increasingly difficult to define the doctrine. The old certainties had disintegrated: socialism had become decentered.

I have in this chapter tried to illuminate the process of enrichment and fragmentation by focusing on two cases that raised very different questions—the feminist and green movements.

Feminist Socialism

If equality, cooperation, and social solidarity are its core values, it might appear self-evident that socialism would regard the role and position of women in society as of critical importance. However, the record of socialism on these issues has often been quite inadequate, particularly in relation to the domestic sphere and sexuality.

Some of the early socialists made a real attempt to integrate male/ female roles and relationships into their thought and practice. As part of his opposition to "religious superstition," the nineteenth-century utopian socialist Robert Owen opposed Christian notions of marriage and regarded the traditional family unit as a barrier to cooperation. Owenites devised their own forms of sexual union based on ceremonies emphasizing equality and cooperation. In practice, however, the lives of women in the cooperative communities often remained difficult, as they continued to play the main part in all the traditional female roles, even if these were organized on a communal basis. In his bizarre way, Owen's contemporary, Charles Fourier, had taken sexual emancipation much further, regarding all forms of sexuality as legitimate and seeking to find outlets for them in his phalanxes. However, Marxist theory was to have greater influence over subsequent socialist ideas.

There were references to women in much of Marx's work, and he was certainly conscious of the dual sources of their oppression in the economic and domestic spheres. However, in general he tended to see their position as a reflection of the social and economic system. Under capitalism this was one of subordination, while social revolution would enable them to engage in creative labor. Yet there was no suggestion that women could be agents of this change—a point that Sheila Rowbotham has criticized particularly effectively in "Dear Mr. Marx: A Letter from a Socialist Feminist" (1998). She drew on evidence of the era to show that there was plenty of available material on which Marx could have based a less male-centered view of the working class. A further weakness in Marx's analysis was his categorization of work so as to include only the production of food and material objects, excluding such activities as child-rearing. By assuming the permanence of the division between production and the domestic realm associated with capitalism, he thus incorporated the contemporary hierarchy between men and women into the heart of his economic theory.

After Marx's death, Engels attempted to explain the position of women more fully in *The Origin of the Family, Private Property, and the State* (1884), basing his interpretation on new anthropological studies. It is notable that he took sexual relationships as of primordial importance in male/female roles. However, he argued that the advent of private property and capitalism had reversed the previous situation in which women had been dominant. He claimed that before the family had existed, there had been a situation of entirely free sexual relationships. As blood relatives had been excluded as partners, the number of eligible women in the tribal group had been reduced and men had claimed individual women, leading to the family. However, he maintained that at this time it was the woman who still exercised economic power because reproduction was necessary for the survival of the tribe and because she produced the primary material goods—bedding, clothing, cooking utensils, and so on. All this had changed as the domestication and breeding of animals, controlled by men, became increasingly important economically. As men became dominant in the production process and created a system of private property, the power relationship between the sexes shifted. Men now wanted to pass on their property to their own children and subjugated women, both through sex and through the division of labor within the household. It therefore followed, according to Engels, that the emancipation of women could only come about with the abolition of private property. He did not elaborate very much on this, but the transformation would involve the socialization of domestic labor, the abolition of the family, and the evolution of authentic "sex-love."

As many later feminists would note, there were unexplained assumptions in Engels's interpretation. Why should women have controlled such resources as bedding, clothing, and cooking unless there was already a sexual division of labor before the development of surplus production and private property? And why should men have taken control of animal husbandry? And if it were really true that there was this kind of difference in the gender roles before the advent of private property, how did it follow that the ending of that economic system would necessarily emancipate women? Nevertheless, Marxist thought did combine the two levels of analysis that would be a key aspect of "second-wave" feminism from the 1960s: the conviction that the subordination of women contained both domestic and economic dimensions.

Almost immediately after the Bolshevik Revolution, the new Soviet state established full citizenship for women and equality was rooted in economic independence and the right (and obligation) to work. New labor laws provided for equal pay and other protections, and a new family law addressed the household dominance of fathers, introduced civil marriage and divorce on demand, abolished illegitimacy, and legalized abortion. This was far in advance of any capitalist society, but there were also some early signs of tension.

One prominent Marxist feminist of the era was Clara Zetkin (1857–1933). Having been a leading activist of the SPD and the Second International before 1914, she subsequently became a founder member of the German Communist Party, but in 1921 took charge of the Communist International Women's Secretariat and spent most of the rest of her life in the Soviet Union. However, soon after the Bolshevik Revolution, Lenin admonished her for encouraging women members of the Communist Party to discuss sexual matters, rather than the fact that the "first state of proletarian dictatorship is battling with the counterrevolutionaries of the whole world." He thus told her, "I could not believe my ears" when informed that "at the evenings arranged for reading and discussion with working women, sex and marriage problems come first."

Of still greater historical significance was the fate of Alexandra Kollontai (1872–1952), the first Commissar of Social Welfare, who initiated some of the early Bolshevik reforms. Kollontai had written *The Social Basis of the Woman Question* in 1908 before fleeing Russia for Western Europe, where she had remained until 1917. During her exile, she had written various articles arguing that, for psychological reasons, women had internalized their dependency on men and that this could only be overcome with the ending of private property, which was the basis for

Alexandra Kollontai (1872–1952), seen in this undated photograph, was a pioneer of the women's movement from the revolutionary Marxist tradition.

male dominance. She went far beyond Engels in integrating economic and sociopsychological factors in her accounts of the position of women, and some of her proposals for overcoming gender divisions in domestic labor recall Fourier, with whose work she was familiar.

After her return to Russia, she played an active role in the Bolshevik Revolution, and in 1920 she headed a special department within the Communist Party (the *Zhenotdel*) devoted to women's issues. Until 1922, she organized nurseries, daycare centers, maternity hospitals, and restaurants so that women could be relieved of the double burden at work and at home. She also instructed workers in the *Zhenotdel* to inform people of their rights, protest against abusive male workers, and push for the inclusion of women at all levels of decision-making. In this period, she continued to write about the socialist relationship between women and men, advocating complete abolition of existing family structures in favor of heterosexual love based on attraction and a joint commitment to creating a new society. She also called for the communal upbringing of children and urged communists to revolutionize the family. However, her theories and policies were not well received by other Soviet communists. Many men were suspicious of her new approach, and Kollontai's involvement in the Workers' Opposition movement within the party alienated the party leadership. In 1922, she was dismissed from the *Zhenotdel* and became a Soviet diplomat. Subsequently, her ideas were condemned in the Soviet press as trivial and feminist (a term of abuse), and after 1926 she stopped speaking out on gender-related issues. After her dismissal from the *Zhenotdel*, its activities were channeled into the more traditional "caring" role, with an emphasis on the socialization of housework and childcare, provision of social services, food distribution, and nursing those who had been wounded during the civil war. Subsequently, Stalin outlawed abortion and restricted divorce.

Yet in many respects, the Soviet Union and its satellites remained more advanced in relation to gender than capitalist societies. Thus in the postwar years, comparative statistics of the socialist and Western countries revealed that in terms of higher educational attainment and professional and political status, women in the Soviet bloc countries were far better represented than their counterparts in Western Europe (outside Scandinavia). Soviet communism prided itself on its emphasis on sexual equality, and major efforts were certainly made to overcome aspects of disadvantage. But little or no attention was paid to the issues that Kollontai had raised in relation to the household itself. For example, by 1989, 80.2% of East German children from birth to three were in daycare, and 95.1% between the ages of three and six were at kindergartens (as against 3% and 67.5% in West Germany), but the party appeared to accept that women would continue to play the main role at home. The objective was to enable women "to reconcile the demands of their job still more successfully with their duties toward child and family." The assumption that the personal was not political was deeply embedded in the consciousness, and perhaps also the theory, of most communists.

The record of social democracy in general was at least as unsatisfactory. In many countries, the most prominent early feminists had been middle-class liberals, who had sought civil and political equality through universal suffrage. Second International socialists had often been ambivalent about allying with them, instead emphasizing the need to emancipate working-class women through employment outside the home. Furthermore, even when socialist theory sounded progressive, the practices of the parties were often highly conservative: on the one hand, women were regarded as politically backward because they were not involved in work and trade unions; on the other hand, it was implied that they should be in the home and barred from all kinds of work for which they were seen to be unsuited. During both world wars, women were brought into the labor force in jobs previously reserved for men, but were subsequently pushed back into more traditional roles, with social democrats generally taking the same line on this as other political parties. And while the development of welfare states certainly benefited working-class women economically, the systems assumed that the male would be the breadwinner while the female would continue to occupy the domestic role. This was quite explicit in the British case, where William Beveridge (1879–1963), the architect of the postwar welfare state, asserted that "during marriage most women will not be gainfully employed." Nor had most social democrats much sympathy with those who had emphasized the personal and sexual aspects of the oppression of women. In general, the male-dominated labor movements tended to view those who advanced such ideas as middle-class feminists, whose preoccupations had no relevance for most women.

Yet after the Second World War, the position of women in advanced capitalist societies changed very considerably, particularly with the vast increase in female employment. Educational opportunities increased and, with them, higher aspirations conflicted with prevailing assumptions; time-saving devices in the home provided a little more time for other activities; and new forms of contraception finally removed the fear of pregnancy from sex. Such changes were to culminate in "second-wave feminism" in the late 1960s.

The movement for women's liberation in this period contained a whole range of political positions, but many socialist feminist thinkers now took issue with Engels's account of the position of women. In the

Simone de Beauvoir (1908–86), whose book *The Second Sex* (1949) was a major influence over feminist thought in the postwar period, appears in this 1947 photograph.

most influential early postwar text, *The Second Sex* (1949), Simone de Beauvoir (1908–86) argued that women had been regarded as "the other" in a male-dominated world and that there was no reason to assume that the abolition of private property would overcome this. As she put it:

> If the human consciousness had not included . . . an original aspiration to dominate the Other, the invention of the bronze tool could not have caused the oppression of women.

De Beauvoir regarded socialism as a precondition for female emancipation, but her position was criticized by many later feminists for accepting the male definition of the world rather than seeking to recast it, for she argued that the way for women to transcend their "otherness" was by engaging fully in traditional masculine pursuits.

A more rigorous examination of Marxist theory was offered by Juliet Mitchell (1940–) in "Women: The Longest Revolution" in *New Left Review* (1966). She suggested that the oppression of women arose from the ideological sphere, for the assumptions used to justify their domestic role were based in the dominant ideas. Their exploitation, in contrast, was based on their position as workers in the capitalist system. This meant that socialism would not automatically resolve the position of women since there needed to be an ideological revolution as well as transformation in the system of production. This was a form of "dual systems theory," for it suggested that the subordination of women arose from both the economic system (capitalism) and a whole set of practices and assumptions (ideology). In other words, Engels's interpretation might be regarded as a necessary part of the explanation, but not sufficient. However, there were others who were arguing that the Marxist account had no relevance at all, and here a key text of the era was *Sexual Politics* (1971) by Kate Millett (1934–). She argued that the relationship between the sexes was based on power and sustained by the ideology and social structure of "patriarchy," irrespective of the economic structure.

Socialists, particularly Marxists, were predisposed to resist this kind of interpretation, but it is here that the experience of 1968 and its aftermath became so relevant. The dominant ideology of the movement of 1968 was one of participatory democracy and a resistance to traditional hierarchies and organizations. Yet, as Eley puts it:

In 1968, girlfriends and wives were present with their men. They made the coffee and prepared the food, wrote the minutes and kept the books. They handled the practical tasks, while decision-making, strategizing, and taking the limelight stayed with the men. Flagrantly contradicting the antihierarchical and participatory ideals of the 1968 movements, this taken-for-granted status soon led to anger.

The aftermath tended to inflame this further, when women who had been radicalized by the New Left and the movement of 1968 joined revolutionary Marxist parties, but also tended to experience subordination to men and male-dominated structures and practices there.

The result was the development across much of Western Europe and the USA of an active women's movement that adopted a new form of politics. This included some high-profile publicity events, including a protest at the Miss World event in 1970, but its most characteristic form was that of small groups of women raising issues of concern and supporting one another in collective activities. A typical approach, derived in part from the U.S. black consciousness movement, was of "consciousness-raising," where women were encouraged to share their experiences, gain more confidence to express their views, and participate in collective decision-making. The best-known slogan encapsulating the approach was "the personal is political." This could have been Clara Zetkin's riposte to Lenin, for it was based on the assumption that issues of sexuality, relationships, and experiences in the home were as "political" as, for example, questions of economic power. However, this did not mean that the more traditional issues were ignored. Campaigns for trade union rights and against low, or unequal, pay for women, and wider social, economic, and

On December 22, 1970, a group of protesters gathered in London to protest what they viewed as the sexist and exploitative Miss World beauty pageant. The contest was founded in 1951 and continues to this day.

political inequalities were also integral concerns. "Consciousness-raising" sought to make connections between apparently personal matters and the social structures in which they were based, and another major concern was with cultural and media representations of women. Finally, the typical structure was more one of networks than of formal organization, as was implied in the term "movement." There was a strong reaction against the proceduralism and hierarchy associated with formal institutions, including parties and trade unions. Instead, there was an emphasis on local actions combined with some national and transnational campaigns on particular issues. For example, a movement to "reclaim the night" to stop sexual violence developed from an International Tribunal of Crimes against Women in Brussels in 1976 and was followed by action in several countries.

Inevitably, the women's movement contained its fair share of problems. There were always political divisions, both between non-socialist and socialist feminists and between the different types of socialists, and these tended to grow rather than diminish by the late 1970s. Some disputes concerned the issue of whether men could play a role at all in the movement, and collective action was also undermined by the attempt of some of the revolutionary Marxist groups to take control—a strategy that was facilitated by the very flexibility and participatory nature of the decision-making. Furthermore, some groups of women from ethnic minorities and the manual working classes felt they were being excluded and sometimes established their own movements. Finally, the development of "identity politics" and postmodernism in the 1980s led to yet more fragmentation in both theories and practices. This ultimately led the women's movement to dissipate, with a tendency for some sections to work more closely with established political parties and public services. The results were mixed and, although there had been substantial progress in comparison with the situation in the early 1960s, by the early twenty-first century no country had yet fulfilled the aspirations of second-wave feminism in relation to the domestic sphere, the world of work, or the social status and representation of women. Indeed, a study published by the Future Foundation in July 2003 suggested that, in Britain at least, the whole concept of feminism was now viewed negatively, even though its demands were still perceived as highly relevant. However, the impact in relation to traditional conceptions of socialism was of fundamental, and probably irreversible, importance.

Fundamental questions had been raised about the deeper sources of the oppression of women and the ways in which these might be overcome. Feminist thought itself developed a whole range of interpretations of the sources of women's subordination, and necessitated a broadening of socialist theories. But whatever theory or combination of theories is accepted, it has become increasingly difficult to make credible claims that Marxism provides a sufficient explanation for the role of women in society, and this realization influenced many socialist feminists.

For example, during the 1970s Mitchell and Rowbotham appealed to psychoanalytical concepts both for an understanding of how and why sexual differences became so important and of how the oppression of women might be overcome, making an attempt to reconcile Marxism and psychoanalysis. This search for a synthesis implied a form of Marxism that was much more open-ended and flexible than that promulgated by most of the revolutionary parties. As Rowbotham also suggested, Marxism was a valuable means of understanding the interactions between historical transformations and people's lives, but its existing shape had itself been made by the forces and central dilemmas confronting socialists in the past. The emergence of the women's movement had shown the underdevelopment of Marxism on relations between the sexes and the connection between this and women's subordination within the Left. Feminism therefore required a remaking of Marxism.

The concern here is neither to explore this "remaking," nor to delve more deeply into feminist thought. The point is rather to suggest that through the women's movement, socialist feminists brought a new approach that inevitably affected theory itself, for the integration of the personal and public spheres was also brought into this realm. This tended to remove the apparent certainty of existing theories—perhaps particularly Marxism—as it became legitimate to introduce doubts and qualifications into the discussions. Furthermore, as Rowbotham also noted, it was not only the apparent certainty of the theory (and the theorists) that was problematic, but that the whole idiom in which Lenin had argued (and she could have extended this to parts of Marx and Engels too) was highly militaristic. In her view, the status of theory, the manner in which it was expressed, and the notion that it should be promoted by an austere revolutionary vanguard were alienating to most women. Rowbotham was concentrating particularly on Marxist theory and revolutionary parties, but many of these strictures applied equally to the kinds of theory utilized by social democrats, for example, in discussions of competitive economics.

The impact of feminism on traditional notions of socialist organization was equally profound. Clearly, there were crucial differences between social democratic parties, in which electoral considerations were often dominant, and those of Marxist parties, intent on revolutionary change. But both were based on formal structures, procedures, and hierarchies to which the feminist movement (like the movements of 1968) was generally opposed, preferring an emphasis on participation, learning from experience, and local activity.

Second-wave feminism therefore challenged both existing theories and practices and, in so doing, contributed to the "decent ring" of socialism. As already noted, this was just one of the many movements that chipped away at traditional conceptions of socialism in the simultaneous process of enrichment and fragmentation. Ecology raised further crucial questions.

united nations
[cli]mate change conference
Nusa Dua - Bali, Indonesia, 3-14 December 2007

Green socialism is a relatively recent phenomenon, sparked by a late-twentieth-century awareness of the economic and political importance of conserving the world's natural resources. One large-scale effort at setting standards for conservation was the 2007 climate-change conference in Bali, Indonesia, sponsored by the United Nations and attended by representatives of more than 180 countries.

Green Socialism

In 1962, when Rachel Carson published *Silent Spring*, concern about environmental degradation through the excessive use of pesticides was a rather esoteric issue and discussions of "ecology" took place only within biology. Meanwhile, it was generally assumed by both Right and Left that economic growth was desirable. By the end of the century, the situation had been transformed. The Kyoto Protocol on climate change in 1997 and the subsequent refusal of the American administration (in 2001) to adhere to the treaty made headline news throughout the world.

By then, scientific debates about the depletion of natural resources and the threat to ecosystems had permeated social, political, and economic discussions. Discourse about sustainability therefore now often replaced that of simple growth.

In principle, ecological arguments could be compatible with a wide range of political positions. For example, an extreme right-wing authoritarian solution could be to seek to establish dictatorships in the richest states, which deployed military power against developing countries so as to preserve the finite global natural resources for their own use. Political perspectives of this kind would certainly threaten socialism, but they would not have challenged it. However, the Green politics that emerged in the latter part of the twentieth century tended to be on the Left. Ecological thought thus raised questions for socialism, while the emergence of Green movements also challenged it in terms of organization and practice. The discussion here focuses mainly on theoretical questions, but the practical impact is also addressed briefly at the end of the section.

Although ecology became an issue of political importance in the last part of the twentieth century, many of its central concerns—the rural and urban environment, health, nature, food—have been raised periodically since the Industrial Revolution. What is new is the urgency of the issue, having really been realized with the publication in 1972 of both the highly influential report by the Club of Rome, *The Limits to Growth*, and "Blueprint for Survival" in the *Ecologist*. A plethora of subsequent studies, including the Brundtland Report, *Our Common Future* (1987), reinforced the conclusions, showing the extent and interrelationship of the problems, but by then there was widespread acceptance of the "message" that, unless there were very fundamental changes in attitudes, behavior, and policies, existing forms of life upon the planet would be threatened.

Ecological thought urges a qualitative change in the whole relationship between human beings and the rest of the natural world by introducing two key considerations. First, it rejects, or at least fundamentally questions, the pursuit of growth as a primary economic objective. Second, because of the conviction that current policies may have devastating and irreparable consequences for the planet itself, it highlights the needs of future generations. This means that issues of justice do not simply concern contemporary social relationships, but that those who live now must also take account of the interests of their successors when, for example, they deplete nonrenewable sources of energy.

Andrew Dobson also draws a distinction between environmentalism and ecologism:

> Environmentalism argues for a managerial approach to environmental problems, secure in the belief that they can be solved without fundamental changes in present values or patterns of production and consumption and ecologism holds that a sustainable and fulfilling existence presupposes radical changes in our relationship with the non-human natural world, and in our mode of social and political life.

He argues that environmentalism can never be sufficient to bring about the kind of transformation required for the survival of the planet and does not constitute "Green thought." Yet the distinction between environmentalism and ecologism seems much less clear than he implies. If consumers en masse bought organic food and boycotted genetically modified products, chose public transport rather than private car use, recycled all rubbish, and heated their houses through solar energy, the effects could be considerable. Similarly, legislation to bring about changes of this kind could force companies to shift their investment into ecologically sensitive products. If this took place throughout the rich countries, would this amount to the kind of fundamental transformation sought by the authors of *The Limits to Growth*? Or does this scale of qualitative change require nil growth and the complete abandonment of current patterns of social and economic life in advanced industrial societies? Obviously, the greater the degree of transformation envisaged, the greater would be the challenge to existing political doctrines, including socialism. If environmentalism and ecologism merge into one another like colors in the rainbow, it is also clear that there are many shades of green, some of which would regard the changes mentioned above as very significant. Here the term "green" will be used to represent the whole environmental/ecological spectrum, rather than solely its dark green (ecological) end.

This photograph, taken in September of 1986, shows policemen observing two environmental activists who had scaled an eleven-story building across the street from the offices of the World Bank in Washington, D.C., to hang a large banner of protest on its facade. The demonstrators, belonging to the Rainforest Action Network, claimed that the world's tropical rain forests were being stripped away in the name of economic development.

Green thought presents a greater challenge to some forms of socialism than others. Many of the utopian socialists in the first half of the nineteenth century wanted to recreate the rural communities that capitalist industrialization was undermining, and even Robert Owen was wedded to the idea of small-scale production. Probably only

Saint-Simon was an enthusiastic supporter of industrialism per se. Similarly, the anarchists Proudhon and Bakunin opposed capitalism partly because they believed that it was destroying more "natural" human communities based on cooperative relationships in the countryside. Although most socialists in European societies subsequently became reconciled to industrial society, these earlier traditions certainly continued to exist. For example, the guild socialist movement in early twentieth-century Britain sought to combine the notion of medieval guilds of crafts with modern trade unionism. It was one of its thinkers, A. J. Penty (1875–1937), who coined the term "post-industrial society" and called for a drastic reduction of large-scale industry and the end of the overpowering state in favor of small-scale production within communes. More generally, there have always been socialists who have attached particular importance to the concerns that are now associated with the Green movement, including conservation, the development of sensitive environmental planning, and a whole range of "quality of life" issues. However, Green thought has provided a major challenge to the two dominant forms of socialism—social democracy and communism.

As shown in the earlier chapters, as the twentieth century progressed, social democracy came to believe that there was no need to overthrow capitalism in order to achieve benefits for the working classes. Indeed, its period of maximum achievement, in the so-called long postwar boom, had depended upon the success of the system to which it had been ostensibly opposed. Economic growth made it possible to provide relatively generous welfare expenditure, for this could then be financed from taxation derived from increases in income. Similarly, full employment had appeared unproblematic with the expansion of domestic and international markets for ever more commodities. The publication of *The Limits to Growth* coincided with the downturn in economic activity in the major capitalist economies in the early 1970s, but social democrats saw the solution as increased government expenditure to restore full employment, and they were certainly not ready for an argument that seemed to suggest that still bigger dangers lay in renewed growth.

Nor was communism any more receptive to the suggestion that ecological imperatives demanded fundamental changes. Under Stalin, rapid growth through industrialization had been the main goal of the system and, although the method (forced labor camps) had subsequently changed, the objective remained, with Krushchev rashly boasting that the Soviet Union would outstrip the economies of the capitalist world by the end of the twentieth century. Manufacturing industry in the whole bloc was also notoriously toxic, and this disregard for the environmental aspects of industrial expansion was certainly one of the causes of the nuclear disaster at Chernobyl in the Ukraine in 1986. Nor was the record elsewhere in the communist world very different (and even in the early twenty-first century, the communist/capitalist system in China appears determined to achieve rapid industrial expansion without due sensitivity to the predictable dangers of its current policies).

Given the priority that both social democracy and communism placed on industrial growth, it was highly unlikely that either would welcome the evidence assembled by Green campaigners from the 1970s onward. The early reactions were therefore either to ignore the evidence or to dismiss it as antisocialist propaganda. An accusation from more traditional socialists was that the Green emphasis on "post-materialism" was fine for the middle classes, but had little relevance for those living in deprived inner-city areas in capitalist countries or for those without drinking water, food, or shelter in developing countries. This charge was

On April 26, 1986, reactor 4 at the Chernobyl nuclear power plant, near Pripyat, Ukraine, exploded. According to *National Geographic*, the fallout contained four hundred times more radioactivity than resulted from the bombing of Hiroshima. This photograph of the abandoned city of Pripyat, with the plant in the distance, was taken in January of 2007.

well placed in the sense that those suffering from acute deprivation might not see the solution in terms of Green policies (but nor, of course, might they see it in socialism). However, outright rejection of ecological arguments became untenable because of the weight of evidence; because the main challenge came from left-inclined Green parties and movements, which shared the socialist belief in equality as a goal; and because campaigns also took place against the damage caused by toxic waste and environmental degradation in working-class areas.

The dominant forms of socialism have therefore needed to reexamine some key assumptions. The traditional claim had been that the current capitalist system was unequal and unjust, but that it would be possible to establish a socialist system that would maintain (and extend) the advantages of capitalist productivity while ending its ills. Such ideas had also characterized attitudes to the world as a whole, with the supposition that enhanced production would mean that global redistribution could be brought about without reductions in living standards in the wealthy countries. Confidence in this view has now been undermined by the ecological evidence, and there can be few people who genuinely believe that the lifestyles (for example, in terms of the use of nonrenewable energy) currently enjoyed by the average family unit in the United States could be achieved globally. To what extent was the belief in unlimited production inherent in the dominant socialist theories?

Marx has often been viewed as a source for such beliefs, and several passages in his work seem to imply ever-increasing productive possibilities following the abolition of capitalism. One of the most powerful ecological critiques of Marxism was made by Rudolf Bahro (1935–), who had been a committed communist in East Germany and later a fundamentalist and visionary figure in Green politics in West Germany. He argued that for Marx socialism was a classless industrial society, and "the industrial aspect of this was to be more or less unproblematically the legacy of capitalism." After quoting a passage from *The Communist Manifesto* which seemed to regard the domination of the whole world market "by the rapid improvement of all instruments of production" as positive, Bahro wrote:

> We can no longer share the spirit in which this was written. Anyone
> who has lived in Eastern Europe has an experience that goes beyond

all theory: industrialism, productivism, Fordism, etc. obstruct the socialist exit rather than lead to it. And the suspicion has arisen in the meantime that [this] . . . happens with every known kind of industrialization, so that the means generally gobbles up the end, which was to have been freedom, love, happiness for all.

He also made it clear that he regarded the Marxist theoretical tradition itself, rather than the East European application of it, as culpable:

Marxists have so far rarely considered that humanity has not only to transform its relations of production, but must also fundamentally transform the entire character of its mode of production.

However, Kate Soper has argued persuasively that other readings of Marx are also plausible. In 1991 she suggested that Marxism is more consistent with ecology than is social democracy because the latter is dependent upon capitalism. For if the capitalist system is based on commodity production and growth to sustain profitability, social democracy cannot make a decision to limit industrial expansion without undermining the growth on which the welfare system is dependent. However, she suggests that Marxism can be wedded to Green objectives because it both explains the productive drive of the capitalist system and provides the basis for a socialist society to take alternative decisions about sufficiency and leisure. Soper argues that her view of a socialist society deciding to seek greater spiritual development by spending less time working, accepting a lower level of material comfort, and spending longer on (ecologically sound) intellectual and leisure pursuits is consistent with Marx's writings. However, even if the theoretical compatibility between Marxist and Green socialism is accepted, this does not resolve such key questions as to how an ecologically friendly society could be achieved or what it would look like.

Clearly the socialist critique of capitalism has always involved the view that a system driven by the pursuit of profit will subordinate other considerations to this goal and also that it creates unnecessary and wasteful commodities at the expense of needs. However, this obviously begs the question: what is a need? Clearly, needs—or at least many of them—are historically and socially determined. We all need food, drink, and warmth, but people in advanced capitalist countries might also believe that they need the choices offered by supermarkets and restaurants, central heating, a car, and a long list of other "essential" items.

Residents of wealthy Western nations like the United States, accustomed to seeing supermarket shelves stocked with what seems like acres of fresh fruit, vegetables, and meat, were perhaps shocked in late 1990 to see photographs like this one from the Soviet Union, which at the time was experiencing severe shortages of even the most basic items.

The fact that Soviet bloc countries appeared to be concerned only with meeting basic needs was an element in the increasing unpopularity of the system, particularly as Western television and films beamed capitalist consumerism to their peoples. It is extremely difficult theoretically to distinguish between wants and needs, particularly, of course, when commodity production and advertising try to convert the former into the latter. Marcuse's emphasis in *One-Dimensional Man* on the way in which advanced capitalist societies manufacture a particular kind of uniform consciousness is illuminating in this context.

Consumption is part of a whole lifestyle embedded in a particular form of society, and it is widely argued that the reduction of material "wants" cannot be brought about without social transformation. While the dominant forms of socialism viewed the necessary transformation primarily through the prism of class relations, many Green thinkers, including Bahro, have wanted to recreate the small communities or communes sought by anarchists and early socialists in the belief that it is only at this level that more frugal lifestyles will be pursued. Yet there are surely good reasons to be skeptical about the restoration of small-scale communities, not only because this seems improbable, but also for theoretical reasons. Martin Ryle points out that it is unlikely that the commune will be able to produce essential medical equipment and that, in any case, both coordination and egalitarian distribution systems require states or statelike entities beyond the local. An alternative approach has been to argue that the solution does not so much lie in changing social organization in territorial terms, but in the whole nexus of relationships between work, leisure, and consumption. André Gorz (1924–2007) has made a very important theoretical contribution in this area.

The French philosopher André Gorz (1924–2007), seen in this 1980s photograph, was the cofounder of *Le Nouvel Observateur*, a weekly French newsmagazine, and was the author of nineteen books.

Gorz was a highly original thinker, who is difficult to categorize. Although his conclusions are now far removed from traditional Marxism, he could still be regarded as a "neo-Marxist" in his theoretical framework and approach. Ecology had been a central theme in his ideas since the mid-1970s, and he emphasized the extent to which the mass of the population is stifled within the world of work. Unlike many Greens, he embraced some of the most advanced technology, claiming that this could bring about greater autonomy through a reduction in the working week. Since the majority of jobs are both boring and enslaving, he regarded this possibility, with a guaranteed minimum income, as potentially liberating, for it provides an opportunity for more autonomous activities, including socially useful pursuits that would benefit others. This would enable people to develop their personalities in a rounded way and simultaneously save the environment from the devastation wrought by an economy dominated by the pursuit of growth. Commodity production and consumption could simultaneously be reduced, with society constructed around a mixture of part-time work, useful social activity, and leisure time.

None of these more radical ecological proposals could be implemented at all easily, but Green pressures have certainly influenced the introduction of some measures near the "environmental management" end of the scale. Many of these have been introduced through legislative regulation and, in the British context, the EU has played a major role in forcing higher standards than would otherwise have been chosen. However, it remains questionable how far changes in behavior and aspiration within capitalist societies can be brought about without reference to the price mechanism. It is, for example, notable that in Britain the use of private cars only began to drop when the government used a tax mechanism to increase the real price of fuel between 1997 and 2000. However, after a protest, the fuel escalator was dropped and car usage increased. This raises major issues for ecological socialists, for indirect taxation of this kind is often inegalitarian.

At the other end of the scale, ecologism faces the same theoretical problem that socialism confronted much earlier as to whether it is a revolutionary or reformist ideology, but it is much more difficult for it to locate the potential revolutionaries than it was for Marxism. Gorz attempted to do so with his category of a "non-class of non-workers," including the unemployed and those in marginal and temporary employment, arguing that they have the least stake in current society and are therefore the most predisposed to favor an ecological alternative. But his view is not widely shared. In 2004 Soper put forward a more plausible proposal, based on electoral politics, in which Green socialists should highlight the joys

> of a consumption less troubled by the knowledge of its socially exploitative and ecologically destructive impact. We need visions of a future consumption built around ecologically less damaging methods of farming and commodity production, the pleasures of unpolluted air and water . . . the expansion of free time, the promotion of cultural and aesthetic modes of self-realization . . .

The idea that a more ecological lifestyle would offer greater pleasures is certainly more alluring than presenting it as a dour necessity to avoid catastrophe. But Green socialists will face an uphill battle in attempting to convince industrial workers and trade unions that irreparable ecological damage is a greater risk than the threat to employment that could follow a fundamental change in the economy.

Whether or not radical ecological proposals are practical politics in the foreseeable future, the Green critique of both social democracy and communism has certainly had an impact upon contemporary socialist thought, forcing a reconsideration of earlier traditions.

Green political practice has also challenged the dominant traditions of socialism. Many Greens have suggested that their political approach is derived from their ecology. For example, the American Green writer Charlene Spretnak argued:

> Human systems may take from Nature lessons concerning interdependence, diversity, openness to change within a system,

flexibility, and the ability to adapt to new events or conditions outside the system.

With that model, one can easily guess that Green politics eschews human systems—whether economic, political, or social—that are rigidly constructed around an ideal of tightly centralized control. Rather Green politics advocates decentralizing political and economic power so that decisions and regulations over money are placed at the smallest scale (that is, the level closest to home) that is efficient and practical.

However, since many activists had been involved in the 1968 movements and were already committed to decentralization, participatory democracy, and nonhierarchical organizations, it seems very likely that such experiences, rather than ecological theory per se, influenced their political approach. In any case, they acted as a new social movement and challenged mainstream politics from the Left. Scientific arguments about ecological damage to the planet may have provided a general perspective, but this was also reinforced by immediate problems and issues, leading to campaigns against nuclear power stations and nuclear weapons, motorways, fast food chains, and so on.

A primary concern of the German Greens, when they suddenly emerged as a significant political force in the early 1980s, was thus the absence of radicalism in the SPD. Of course, the Greens subsequently revealed the same kinds of internal division that had historically led to schisms within traditional left-wing parties, and in 1998 and 2002 they would even enter a coalition with the middle-of-the-road SPD government under Gerhard Schroeder. However, this does not alter the

In 1993, Alliance 90, a coalition of political groups, merged with the German Green Party to form Alliance 90/The Greens. This photograph was taken at the party's 2005 convention in Oldenburg, Germany.

fact that their ranks included many New Left activists and that both their policies and general approach place them on the left of the political spectrum, with some overtones of anarchism in their genealogy. In recent years, it has therefore been evident that many young people, who would previously have adhered to social democratic, communist, or Trotskyist parties, have been attracted to the Greens. The Green electoral challenge to mainstream parties has generally been contained at less than 10% of the vote in most European countries (although they exceeded this percentage in Finland, Luxemburg, and the Netherlands in the 1999 Euro elections). However, whether as single parties or as part of a broader alliance, the Greens have certainly played a role in redefining the Left.

This means that, while the Green challenge to socialism was ostensibly about ecological theory, it was actually much wider than this for, as with feminism, it also concerned the definition and practice of politics itself. Thus, whereas the previous assumption of both social democracy and communism was that socialism could be defined by, and achieved through, a party that would aggregate all the relevant issues, this logic is no longer accepted. Once again, as with feminism, the enrichment that Green thought and practice could offer to socialism simultaneously contributed to its ideological and organizational fragmentation.

Beyond the Fragments?

Both individually and in combination, feminists and greens (and several other movements) challenged the dominant forms of socialism by raising fundamental issues about its theory and practice. For traditionalists, such developments were alarming, for fragmentation could threaten to undermine socialism both as a coherent world outlook and in its organizational forms. However, the pressures that produced these new ideas and movements suggested inadequacies in the existing ideological and organizational structures. A text from 1979 that sought to combine feminism and socialism is very illuminating in its attempt to define a new approach.

In *Beyond the Fragments* (1979), three socialist feminists in Britain, Sheila Rowbotham, Lynne Segal, and Hilary Wainwright, directly confronted the fact that socialism was no longer unified in doctrinal or organizational terms, but contained several movements and ideas. The most substantial essay, by Rowbotham, "The Women's Movement and Organizing for Socialism," specifically dealt with these issues. Her particular concern was to argue that the concept of a Leninist party was incompatible with socialist feminism and other new movements, but many of her insights also apply to social democracy. She thus argued for the creation of an organization with forms of internal association that would actively overcome discrimination through open expression of difference between the particular groups:

> For if every form of oppression has its own defensive suspicions, all the movements in resistance to humiliation and inequality also discover their own wisdoms. We require a socialist movement in which there is freedom for these differences, and nurture for these wisdoms. This means that in the making of socialism people can develop positively their own strengths and find ways of communicating to one another what we have gained, without the transcendent correctness which Leninism fosters.

Yet her critique of the idea of a monolithic party did not mean that she believed that the goal of socialism should be replaced by a whole set of entirely distinct social movements:

> When the black movement in the late sixties followed by women and gay people asserted the idea of oppression which could include the cultural and personal experience of being subordinated as a group as well as economic and social inequalities, it was an important corrective to the emphasis within the left on class and economic exploitation. . . . But arguing in terms of a series of separate "oppressions" can have an ironic consequence. We can forget that people are more than the category of oppression. . . . We thus have the means of seeing people as victims but not the means of seeing the sources of power which all subordinated groups have created.

The argument was that connections needed to be made between the various movements, with the previous polarities superseded. She could not suggest an ideal new model of a nonauthoritarian organization, but

> a collective awakening to a constant awareness about how we see ourselves as socialists, a willingness to trust as well as criticize what we have done, a recognition of creativity in diversity and a persistent quest for open types of relationships to one another and to ideas as part of the process of making socialism.

In the long run, she suggested that new forms of socialist organizing, which could grow from such a practice and bring together these efforts toward a different politics, would be necessary.

The intention, also emphasized by Wainwright, was to find a socialist way of going "beyond the fragments." Socialist feminists and socialist greens, as well as many others in the new social movements of the era, opposed both the organizational and ideological forms of communism and social democracy and believed that pluralism enriched both the theory and practice of socialism. Such diversity became an enduring feature of the life of the Left. There were also some evident continuities between the social movements that developed in the 1970s and 1980s and those demanding global justice in the early twenty-first century. This pluralism undoubtedly enriched socialism, recalling the nineteenth century, when many traditions had coexisted. However, it also meant fragmentation during a period in which socialism as a whole appeared to be threatened. The implications of this will be considered in the final chapter.

FOUR

Socialism Today and Tomorrow

•

IN THE EARLY 1900S, THE PARTIES of the Second International were confident that socialism would be established during the coming century; few share this confidence a hundred years later. While it is scarcely surprising that liberal and conservative commentators have pronounced the "death of socialism," it is also notable that several on the Left have apparently come to a similar conclusion. This mood is understandable as the outlook appears bleak. By the year 2005, few communist regimes were still in existence. In China and Vietnam, single-party states continued, but the economic system was increasingly based on the capitalist market; in North Korea, a "totalitarian" personality cult remained but much of its population was in dire poverty; and in Cuba there were doubts as to whether the

Even in a communist nation such as China, the spread of American-style capitalism is evident—especially in photographs like this one, taken in 2007.

regime would survive once Castro died. Meanwhile, social democracy had increasingly departed from traditional forms of socialism, and in much of Europe the extreme Right and the forces of xenophobia and racism were apparently on the rise. Certainly, the Left could draw some comfort from the development of movements for global justice, the victory of the Workers' Party in the Brazilian general election in the autumn of 2002, and the massive international demonstrations in February 2003 opposing the imminent war in Iraq. However, even the most wildly optimistic would probably acknowledge that, with the United States as the sole superpower and committed to spreading its model of capitalism across the globe, this was certainly a cold climate for socialists.

Later in the chapter, it will be argued that the feeling of gloom is unwarranted. However, it is first necessary to examine some of the fundamental changes that became evident after the mid-1970s, which account for the current difficulties experienced by all forms of socialism. These transformations need to be examined before future possibilities can be discussed.

The Malaise of Social Democracy

It is widely agreed that the heyday of social democracy in the advanced capitalist societies of Western Europe coincided broadly with the long post-war boom from the late 1940s until the 1970s. As noted in Chapter 2, the so-called "Keynesian" settlement, associated with the ideas of the British economist John Maynard Keynes, had involved government intervention in the economy to maintain full employment and high levels of social expenditure. This had neither operated in a uniform way across the region nor depended exclusively upon social democratic parties, for other parties also played a role in establishing and upholding this system.

Nevertheless, the association between Keynesianism and social democracy was of particular importance and had several dimensions.

The first was that of ideological legitimation. Outside Scandinavia, interwar social democracy had little to show for its claim that it was possible to transform capitalism in a socially progressive direction through peaceful, parliamentary means. The establishment of the postwar system appeared to demonstrate the viability of the social democrats' claim. Their definition of socialism became less precise over time, while the claim that it was being achieved gradually through reforms was stated increasingly boldly. Second, the new system strengthened the bargaining role of the organized working class through trade unions, which were able to influence the direction of economic and social policy, and some states operated a system (sometimes known as "corporatism") in which government, capital, and labor were recognized as tripartite interests in an ongoing bargaining relationship.

There were, of course, always strains within this system. For example, the Labour governments in Britain struggled to make any economic and social progress between 1964 and 1970—in theory, at the height of the period when Keynesianism was operating successfully. Nevertheless, these years certainly compared very favorably with the subsequent period. One fundamental reason for the change was economic downturn. During the 1950s and 1960s the average growth rate in the advanced capitalist economies of the OECD was nearly 5% per year, and this was the basis for the rapid increase in social expenditure as a proportion of GDP, particularly in Western Europe. Thus, in 1949 social expenditure averaged 9% of GDP in 13 West European countries, and by 1960 it was still only just above 11%. However, by 1970, it had reached 15.8%, rising to 22.4% by 1977, with the fastest increase, of 5.4 percentage points, in the first half of the 1970s. It was because growth rates were unprecedented that it was possible to maintain full employment and social welfare benefits without undermining profitability or the interests of private capital. Domestic growth in turn depended upon expansion in the international economy, and here the United States played a key role in maintaining an international economic and financial system based on the convertibility of the dollar with gold. This was known as the Bretton Woods system, as it had been conceived at a meeting there in 1944.

In the early 1970s, all this changed, although the exact causality is not agreed. After the Arab-Israeli war in autumn 1973, there was a massive increase in oil prices, coupled with the establishment of a unilateral dollar exchange system, replacing the Bretton Woods mechanisms. This was followed in 1974 by the U.S. abolition of controls on the outflow of

The United Nations Monetary and Financial Conference, held at the Mount Washington Hotel in Bretton Woods, New Hampshire (July 1–22, 1944), brought together representatives of all forty-four Allied nations in an effort to formulate an economic plan for post–World War II reconstruction. Here, the British economist John Maynard Keynes addresses the conference.

capital, leading to an entirely new order with private financial institutions at the center of the international monetary regime. The conventional explanation for this is that the U.S. was unable to uphold the existing system because of its recurrent balance of trade deficits, leading it to abandon the dollar as a reserve currency, ushering in a period of exchange rate instability. However, Peter Gowan has argued plausibly that this was a deliberate strategy by President Nixon that simultaneously liberated the U.S. state from succumbing to its economic weaknesses and pushed the crisis onto its rivals in Europe and Japan. In any case, the decline in economic performance was dramatic. In 1974 the average OECD growth rate was 2%, while in the next year nine OECD economies had negative growth. In 1975 unemployment in the OECD economies was at easily its highest postwar level of fifteen million, but this doubled within the next decade, accompanied by declining investment and profitability, and stagnating disposable income. As Christopher Pierson argues, governments were simultaneously failing to achieve the four major policy objectives on which the postwar order had been based: economic growth, low inflation, full employment, and a favorable balance of trade.

Keynesianism suggested that when there was evidence of a fall in demand in the economy, with the threat of declining employment, governments should increase their own expenditure to counteract the effects of this low phase in the business cycle. However, the situation now differed from that of the interwar period because of the phenomenon of "stagflation"—the combination of economic recession and high inflation. Had there been a general commitment to continue with the postwar system, a coordinated response would no doubt have been possible, but this would have required a political will to undertake the necessary measures. For Keynesianism had depended on governments regarding the maintenance of full employment as a key priority. There was now no international agreement to maintain this in the changed economic circumstances, and it is ironic that a British Labour prime minister, James Callaghan, effectively announced the end of the era when he told the 1976 Party conference:

> We used to think that you could just spend your way out of a recession and increase employment by cutting taxes and boosting government spending. I tell you, in all candor, that the option no longer exists, and that insofar as it did exist, it only worked by injecting a bigger dose of inflation into the economy followed by higher levels of unemployment as the next step.

Three years later, the Thatcher government (effectively in alliance with the U.S.) deliberately sought to create a situation that would permanently remove the existing basis for social democracy. The British acted as pathbreakers, but by the mid-1980s the postwar system was being eroded across Europe. In this respect, the U-turn of François Mitterrand's French socialist government was particularly significant. After a brief period of expansionist policies immediately after taking office, this administration turned toward austerity measures in 1982, apparently burying the idea of Keynesianism in a single country.

The Ideological Battle

By the early 1970s, neoliberal economic thought provided a critique of the Keynesian welfare state, which Pierson has usefully summarized as having the following four elements. First, it was said to be uneconomic, in displacing the necessary disciplines and incentives of the marketplace,

Margaret Thatcher (1925–), who served as British prime minister from 1975 to 1990, formed close political ties with the United States. Thatcher and George H. W. Bush, then vice president under Ronald Reagan, posed for this photograph at Chequers, the prime minister's official country residence, on February 12, 1984.

undermining the incentive of capital to invest and of labor to work. Second, it was unproductive in encouraging the rapid growth of public bureaucracy and in forcing capital and human resources out of the productive private sector of the economy. At the same time, the monopoly of state welfare provision had enabled workers within the public sector to command inflationary wage increases. Third, it was regarded as inefficient since the state's monopoly of welfare provision and sponsorship of the special interests of trade unions led to an inefficient delivery of services and a system geared to the interests of organized producers rather than consumers. This was because of the lack of market disciplines. Finally, it was also condemned as ineffective in failing to eliminate poverty and deprivation, despite the resources devoted to welfare.

Such ideas were constantly propounded from the late 1970s, with an insistence on the superiority of the market over any form of government intervention. This was coupled with the ideological claim that people were being set free to make their own decisions, particularly in purchasing services, and that this liberated them from state bureaucracies. It was claimed that collective, universal provision of uniform services might have been appropriate in the early postwar years of austerity, but that people no longer wanted to be passive recipients of state provision. The neoliberals reinforced their attack on social democrats by claiming that they ("socialists") did not want to liberate people in this way. On the contrary, it was argued that they sought to maintain a dependency relationship from which the state, parties, and trade union bureaucracies, rather than citizens, derived the primary benefits. This ideology probably appealed only to a minority. However, the politicians who were in the vanguard of the "New Right"—notably Reagan and Thatcher— knew what they were doing. Basing their position on some of the insights derived from corporations seeking to attract consumers through "life-style" product marketing, they were aware that there were people in all classes who would respond to a message stressing individual aspirations. Some of them could now be recruited to the Right.

In reality, none of the governments made such inroads into welfare provision as the rhetoric implied. But through partial privatization of state provision, through the development of benefits aimed at flexible labor markets rather than universality, and through their ideological justifications for the changes, they transformed its nature. During the Keynesian era, social democrats had viewed welfare systems as a matter of collective rights or social citizenship. By the mid-1980s, the new conventional wisdom was that individuals could and should take care of themselves rather than relying on the state, and that the costs of welfare needed to be kept under control so that taxation would not be at "prohibitive" levels. Similarly, it had previously been taken for granted that public services should be publicly provided. By the mid-1980s, the tendency was to claim that public provision always needed to be justified, for people were more interested in the quality of the service than its source.

At the time, there was much anxious speculation about the electoral prospects for social democratic parties in the new conditions, but the enduring problem was still more fundamental. For, with the apparent disappearance of the international political economy that had sustained Keynesianism, and the assault on its associated ideological legitimacy, social democrats were in danger of losing their raison d'être.

Social Changes

The ideological onslaught was accompanied by longer-term social and cultural changes. The assumption of Marx that the industrial working

The decline of the manufacturing and industrial sectors of the world economy, and the corresponding rise of the service and information sectors—including financial services—has meant that there are fewer blue collar workers in trade unions than there were in the 1970s. The rise in the number of white-collar workers, like this stock trader, has also been accompanied by a rise in the number of women in the workforce.

class was the basis for socialism had been adopted by the mass parties of the Left since the late nineteenth century. However, there was now much discussion as to whether such parties could survive if they were tied to this sector of the population.

The claim was that the working class was in decline. At the beginning of the 1970s, 42% of the workforce of the European Community worked in blue-collar manufacturing industry. By 1990, 60% were employed in the service sector and only 32.5% in industry (and by the beginning of the twenty-first century, only 16% were in manufacturing industry, while over 75% were employed in the service sector or knowledge-producing industries). This was coupled with a rise in the female workforce, which had reached nearly 40% of the total workforce in 1988, with nearly 75% of women workers in the service sector. The private service sector was less unionized than industry, as was part-time work, in which there had been an increase, mainly among women. In the UK, unionization declined sharply from its peak of 55.4% in 1979 to 37.7% in 1990, and was only 30% by 1997. This picture was not consistent across all countries: as noted in Chapter 2, Sweden certainly defied the downward trend in trade union membership, and trade union density also remained above 70% in Denmark and Finland. Nevertheless, the rise in the service sector and part-time and temporary work was general across all the advanced industrial countries. This was coupled with a shift from the kinds of living and working conditions that were historically associated with the labor movement. The general trend was toward more atomized employment and the dispersal of traditional working-class communities.

Such changes were connected with developments that have already been discussed. The growth of the service sector was expedited by the U.S.-led move to free capital movements and the consequent strengthening of the role of private transnational corporations and monetary institutions. In Britain, at least, the decline in unions dominated by militant manual workers was sometimes deliberately engineered by the government, most notably in the confrontation with the miners in 1984–85. The general power of trade unions was also reduced by institutional changes. Again, this was most obvious in Britain when the Thatcher government simply removed the Trade Union Congress from its previous position as a privileged interlocutor in policy discussions. Yet even apparently progressive reforms aimed at improving working conditions, such as those of the first Mitterrand socialist government in France, tended to undermine the power of the organized working class where the (already low) trade union density of 17.5% in 1980 had dropped to 9.8% ten years later.

Naturally, there has been a sharp debate among socialists and, more particularly, Marxists as to whether any of the above changes mean that there has been a decline in the working class. It may be argued, on the contrary, that there has been an increase, as people in the service sector and the professions have been "proletarianized" and the agricultural and self-employed sectors have declined. There is therefore a far higher percentage of people who live by selling their labor power for wages than has ever been the case before. In theory, all forms of salaried employees may be viewed as part of a single class. There is no reason why male blue-collar workers should have been "objectified" as "the working class," and there are many good reasons (as noted in Chapter 3) for condemning the fact that, historically, this has been the tendency in labor movements. However, there is considerable evidence to suggest that in practice the working class, however defined, was becoming more segmented. Interunion rivalries tended to grow, union alignments with social democratic parties weakened, there was an increasing tendency to class de-alignment, and there was also a reduction in people's self-perception as "working class." Defining all these groups as "working class" did not mean that they would act in the ways predicted by Marx, or even by social democrats. As Geoff Eley has put it:

> Contemporary transformations were not the "death of class" or the "end of the working class" per se. They were the passing of one type of class society, the one that was marked by working-class formation between the 1880s and 1940s and the resulting political alignments, with its apogee in the postwar settlement. As long-term

changes in the economy combined with the attack on Keynesian-ism, the unity of the working class ceased to be available in that old and well-tried form as the natural ground of left-wing politics.

This verdict was already becoming dominant in the literature of the mid-1980s, and this point is perhaps as important as the structural changes that were being described. For socialism has always depended not only on the nature of society at a particular time, but also on the way that it is perceived and interpreted. The transformation in the intellectual climate in this period was particularly dramatic.

Theory and Ideology

It is difficult to evaluate the significance of ideas and theory in generating support for socialism. No doubt intellectuals tend to overestimate their impact, for popular culture and the media certainly play a far greater role in the cultivation of beliefs than academic discussions. In this respect, the Americanization of television and the emergence of multimedia mag-nates are evidently of great importance in helping to explain attitudinal changes in the last quarter of the twentieth century. Nevertheless, as Gramsci in particular noted, intellectuals certainly have importance in creating a climate of opinion. In general, their views might support the mainstream perspectives, but they could also contribute to the creation of a counter-hegemonic project by turning socialism into "common sense."

During the early 1970s, the intellectual climate still reflected the political upsurge of the movements of the New Left and the era of 1968. There had been a growth of interest in Marxism, and even com-paratively abstruse theoretical debates, such as that on the nature of the capitalist state, had generated great interest in the wider academic

The British historian Eric Hobsbawm (1917–) was one of the speakers at the annual Hay Festival of Literature and the Arts in Hay-on-Wye, Wales, in 2009.

community. Certainly, there were bitter controversies within left-wing academic circles, but few argued that the transformations in the world meant that socialism was no longer a viable project. However, during the last quarter of the century many intellectuals did start to say this or, at least, argued that fundamental elements of socialism needed to be completely rethought.

Two texts were of particular importance in ushering in the new intellectual era. Eric Hobsbawm's *The Forward March of Labor Halted?* was first published in *Marxism Today* in September 1978. In theory, it concerned the situation in Britain, but it was evident that it had more general implications and, because of his Communist Party membership and international reputation, it was soon widely known. It was a brief overview of the evolution of the working class in the past one hundred years and, in line with the trends noted above, it concluded that many of the working classes had "lost faith and hope in the mass party of working people." The industrial militancy that had taken place in the early 1970s did not translate into any socialist consciousness and, he suggested:

> We cannot rely on a simple form of historical determinism to restore the forward march of British labor which began to falter thirty years ago. . . . [I]f the labor and socialist movement is to recover its soul, its dynamism, and its historical initiative, we, as Marxists, must do what Marx would certainly have done: to recognize the novel situation in which we find ourselves, to analyze it realistically and concretely, to analyze the reasons, historical and otherwise, for the failures as well as the successes of the labor movement, and to formulate not only what we would want to do, but what can be done.

Two years later, Gorz presented some rather similar conclusions about the working class. *Adieux au Prolétariat* [*Farewell to the Working Class*] was a thoroughgoing, powerful, and extremely provocative neo-Marxist critique of the traditional socialist perspective. The traditional working class, Gorz suggested, was being eroded by technology and fragmentation, and the critical edge to his argument rested on three major claims: that the working class was not a universal class with a "mission" of human emancipation; that individual consciousness was not a part of class consciousness; and that alienation and hierarchy were embedded in the modern state and industry so that the overthrow of capitalism would not cure these problems.

Both these interventions questioning the role of the working class were highly influential, and during this era traditional forms of socialism themselves also came under increasing attack. In particular, postmodernism appeared on the intellectual scene and seemed to threaten some of the central tenets of socialism in general and Marxism in particular. While the Left might dissent from the specific political form of the eighteenth-century Enlightment, most socialists were happy to concur with its assumptions about reason and the growth of understanding and progress. However, they were now confronted with the argument that this was all part of a modernizing project that suppressed other voices. In particular, postmodernists were deeply suspicious of the claims of a universal rationality and of structural theories that purported to explain "reality." As one of its key figures, Jean-François Lyotard, expressed it in *The Post-Modern Condition*, the essence of the approach was "incredulity toward metanarratives," which were said to mask the nature of power and to be repressive. Marxism was certainly such a metanarrative and socialism, more generally, was wedded to the so-called "Enlightenment project."

The problem for socialism was that such currents of thought had resonance because they appeared to correspond to some discernible social and cultural phenomena. The era was increasingly one of identity politics in which a whole range of movements—by women, gays and lesbians, and minority ethnic groups—were stressing the importance of defining their own "meanings" rather than slotting into a role prescribed by a grand theory or narrative. And postmodernism also appeared to relate to other important trends in intercultural relations. For example, European socialists might argue that they sought to emancipate the rest of the world from capitalism and imperialism, but did they not also adhere to a modernist perspective on progress? Were they not committed both to a particular notion of development and to a conception of high Western culture which suppressed indigenous voices?

In one sense, these challenges were simply a continuation of the themes analyzed in Chapter 3. However, while fragmentation was certainly already discernible in the 1970s, it simultaneously led to enrichment. During the 1980s, the emphasis shifted, partly because there was an increasing tendency for postmodernism and identity politics to take an antisocialist form. Perhaps of still greater importance was the fact that these intellectual debates were taking place while the international political economy that had sustained Keynesianism was being radically restructured. While postmodernists might be skeptical about the notion of "reality," their outlook was in conformity with trends in the material world. All these debates still appear very current but, when they began, a crucial series of events had not yet occurred: the collapse of the East European regimes, followed by the disintegration of the Soviet Union.

The Collapse of Soviet Communism

By the time Mikhail Gorbachev became the Soviet leader in 1985, few socialists in capitalist countries continued to believe that Soviet-style communism was a model to emulate. Even most Western communist parties had now generally distanced themselves from Moscow. For many on the Left, the Soviet-led crushing of the Prague Spring in Czechoslovakia in 1968 had dissipated any remaining illusions that a reformed communism, combining equality with democracy, was a likely prospect. In the summer of 1980, some hoped that the strength of the Solidarity movement in Poland might still lead to a socialist democracy there, but this would certainly have taken place outside communist control. In any case, the bizarre combination of military dictatorship and communism established in Poland in December 1981 to prevent Soviet military intervention put paid to any such prospect and, by then, most socialists probably expected very little that was positive from these regimes. Nevertheless, Gorbachev's desperate attempts to reform the system so as to save it reawakened some hopes that there might, after all, be some possibility of fundamental change. It is not possible to discuss the complex reasons for his failure here, but its repercussions for the fate of socialism have obviously been immense.

His decision—certainly not planned in 1985—to let the East European satellites go their own way was evidently of critical importance in precipitating the collapse of the communist regimes. These had always been dependent upon Soviet power and could not have been overthrown without the withdrawal of that support. But the downfall of the regimes in 1989 and 1990 also showed that none of them had sufficient domestic popularity to survive once the Soviet leadership decided that they were

This issue of *Tygodnik Solidarność*, or *Solidarity Weekly*, was published in July of 1981, just before the communist government of Poland declared a state of martial law. Today, Solidarity survives as an active trade union with more than one million members.

no longer needed. At the same time, the Chinese regime's suppression of student protests in Tiananmen Square in June 1989 demonstrated its brutality and implied that it too lacked domestic legitimacy. These dual manifestations of collapse and repression were equally potent images for all those who regarded democracy as an integral part of socialism. The escalating political, economic, and national crises that led to Gorbachev's resignation in December 1991, and the final collapse of the Soviet Union and Soviet communism, constituted the end of an historical era.

As argued above, social democracy was already in the doldrums and traditional socialist thought under challenge before the collapse of communism. Some socialists now claimed that the downfall of the Soviet bloc either made no difference or could even strengthen socialism by removing its association with the Soviet regime. This might have made sense had the general climate of the times been more favorable to socialism, but it was a forlorn hope at this stage. In *Reflections on the Revolution in Europe* (1990), Ralf Dahrendorf expressed the dominant view in an immediate verdict on the significance of the collapse in Eastern Europe:

> [T]he point has to be made that socialism is dead, and that none of its variants can be revived for a world awakening from the double nightmare of Stalinism and Brezhnevism.

Dahrendorf argued that communism was a phenomenon of developing countries that was ultimately self-destructive once a particular economic level had been attained, while social democracy, by tempering the excesses of unconstrained capitalism, had made itself redundant. He concluded that the historical law of Marxism had been inverted, for it was capitalism that succeeded socialism.

On the morning of November 10, 1989, crowds of German citizens helped each other over the Berlin Wall in response to previous day's announcement that East Germany would grant exit visas to those of its residents who wanted to go to the West. East German border guards were unable or unwilling to control the thousands of people who rushed to the wall believing that the border was completely open. Over the course of the following months, the wall was dismantled, and Germany was reunited the following year as communism collapsed in the Soviet bloc.

This argument posed a major challenge to socialists. Moreover, it soon became clear that the ramifications of the collapse were far wider than was immediately obvious, as the subsequent crisis in Cuba, discussed in Chapter 2, demonstrated. Similarly, the U.S. has been able to carve out its "new world order" without any other power providing serious resistance. This has undoubtedly also enabled it to pursue a global open-market strategy far more aggressively than would have been the case during the era of competition with the Soviet Union. Since China has decided to join the international capitalist economy rather than attempt to provide a counter pole of attraction based on an alternative system, no form of socialism has been able to challenge this hegemony. This means that all states, and particularly those in developing countries, are far more exposed to market pressures than was the case during the era of the Cold War competition. This is the situation currently confronting socialists.

Socialism in the Twenty-First Century: Reactions to the Crisis

Socialists have reacted in various ways to the current difficulties. Some have expressed deep pessimism. The trajectory of Perry Anderson, a major figure on the intellectual Marxist Left, epitomizes this mood. In 1962, when he took control of the journal New Left Review, Anderson was exuberant about the new currents of Marxism, particularly in Continental Europe, and expressed the optimism of the contemporary New Left. In 2000, he wrote an article entitled "Renewal," which could equally well have been called "Requiem for Socialism," in which he expressed the following ideas:

> Ideologically, the novelty of the present situation stands out in historical view. It can be put like this. For the first time since the Reformation, there are no longer any significant oppositions—that is, systematic rival outlooks—within the thought-world of the West; and scarcely any on a world scale either . . . Whatever limitations persist to its practice, neo-liberalism as a set of principles rules undivided across the globe: the most successful ideology in world history.

The Right, he insisted, had a fluent vision of the world which had no equivalent on the Left and:

It is unlikely the balance of intellectual advantage will alter greatly before there is a change in the political correlation of forces, which will probably remain stable so long as there is no deep economic crisis in the West. Little short of a slump of interwar proportions looks capable of shaking the parameters of the current consensus.

Yet such prophets of doom simplify reality even when they purport to represent it in the most intellectual, sober, and rational terms. Pessimism is normally based on the myth of a golden age in the past. Certainly, the existence of the Soviet bloc and of Keynesian demand management policies in the West gave both communism and social democracy some power. But it should not be suggested that socialism as a whole was therefore in a healthy state in the late 1950s or early 1960s, for this implies that the models that then existed contained the essence of the doctrine and that subsequent enrichments are somehow trivial in comparison. Anderson does acknowledge the gains made by feminists and ecologists in the advanced world as "the most important elements of human progress in these societies of the last thirty years," but this is little more than an aside that does nothing to offset the overwhelmingly bleak mood. Socialists have sometimes invoked the slogan of "pessimism of the intelligence and optimism of the will," but Ralph Miliband criticized this in the 25th anniversary edition of *New Left Review* in 1985:

> For it tells us that reason dictates the conviction that nothing is likely to work out as it should, that defeat is much more likely than success, that the hope of creating a social order free from exploitation and domination is probably illusory; but that we must nevertheless strive towards it, against all odds, in a mood of

resolute despair. It is a "noble" slogan, born of romantic pathos, but without even the merit of plausibility; for there is not likely to be much striving if intelligence tells us that the enterprise is vain, hopeless, doomed . . .

In Anderson's case it is not even clear that there is an "optimism of the will" and his particular form of realism implies resignation to defeat. It is difficult to reconcile this with the socialist conviction that the inequality and injustice embedded in the capitalist system will always lead to movements of protest and opposition, and that these will contain elements of progress even if they do not lead to nirvana.

A second reaction from the political mainstream has been to attempt to define a "third way," as proposed by Tony Giddens. This, he argued,

Jubilee 2000 was a political movement that urged Western nations to cancel third-world debt by the year 2000. The movement's name recalls Leviticus 25:13: "In the year of this jubile[e] ye shall return every man unto his possession." On December 2, 2000, these marchers in London carried placards urging the British government to eliminate the debt burden for developing countries.

refers to a framework of thinking and policy-making that seeks to adapt social democracy to a world which has changed fundamentally over the past two or three decades. It is a third way in the sense that it is an attempt to transcend both old style social democracy and neoliberalism.

This was based on the claim that traditional socialism had been discredited, but that its goals could be advanced through "modernization." However, close scrutiny of the ideas themselves, let alone of the policies of New Labor, really suggest that this shift constituted a break with socialism. Although the idea certainly attracted interest in most social democratic

Protests against capitalism and inequality—such as this one, held in Pittsburgh, Pennsylvania, on September 25, 2009, on the occasion of the G-20 summit—suggest that socialist ideals are alive and well in many nations throughout the world.

parties (with the partial exception of the French Socialist Party), it is rooted in British experience because the impact of neoliberalism had been greater there than elsewhere. By 1992, when the Thatcherite reforms had gone so far, and the Labour Party had lost four successive general elections, extensive rethinking appeared necessary. In such circumstances, the idea of combining the concept of "society" with an emphasis on service delivery rather than public ownership clearly provided a new basis for support. However, the general emphasis has been on labor flexibility, individual choice, and the importation of both private capital and private sector values into the public sector. Change has also been sought through the imposition of targets and benchmarks, reflecting a managerial approach to policy. This has certainly been coupled with an attempt to alleviate poverty, but it seems that New Labor and, to an extent, European social democracy in general, has reacted to the current difficulties by moving toward liberalism rather than by modernizing socialism.

A third reaction to the difficulties has been to turn to frameworks in which ideas compatible with socialism could be propounded without any reference to it. Instead, new approaches to human rights, citizenship, cosmopolitanism, democracy, and global government (or governance) have become fashionable. Through reorienting these essentially liberal ideas in more radical directions, it became possible to offer a leftist perspective without proposing an explicitly socialist framework. Thus it was argued that each of these concepts needed to incorporate economic, social, collective, and, sometimes, ecological dimensions in order to be realized in a full sense. In this way, elements of socialism could be embedded within the theories and proposals without needing to be acknowledged. There are certainly advantages in such an approach, for it holds the possibility of winning intellectual and political support from those who would not be drawn to a specifically socialist perspective. It also means that it is possible to secure advances in one sphere without necessarily seeking to win battles on all fronts. However, it also has some important disadvantages, which may be illustrated in relation to the concept of human rights.

There is no doubt about the importance of human rights and, in my view, their defense and enlargement should be regarded as an integral part of socialism. Had this always been the case, it would have been more difficult for those who regarded themselves as socialists to have justified the crimes of Stalin on the grounds that the ends justified the means. However, this is not the same as arguing that the concept of human rights—even with the incorporation of socioeconomic and collective rights—is a substitute for socialism.

It was suggested in Chapter 1 that the starting point for socialism was a critique of capitalism combined with a commitment to the creation of an egalitarian society based on the values of solidarity and cooperation. This does not imply acceptance of a holistic and self-contained doctrine purporting to explain everything, but it does suggest some interconnected values, theories, and practices that help to define an outlook on the world. It is, of course, possible that those who derive their judgments from a broad concept of human rights will often reach precisely the same conclusions as socialists. However, their stance is then likely to be contested by theorists who incline to the position that confines human rights to the civil and political spheres. This suggests that traditional ideological differences cannot be transcended by the use of human rights discourse. Similar conclusions follow if the concepts of citizenship, cosmopolitanism, democracy, and global governance are considered. I would therefore argue that socialists should maintain their own doctrine, rather than allow its dissipation into a set of discrete ideas. This does not imply either inflexibility or an unwillingness to acknowledge the importance of such ideas.

A final typical response has been to argue that it is not socialism itself that has been discredited, but only its dominant forms. Trotskyists, who have always seen both social democracy and communism (or "Stalinism") as betrayals, have therefore continued to express apparent confidence that the future is bright if Marxism-Leninism-Trotskyism is now embraced. However, this claim has been made for over seventy years without convincing sufficient numbers of its plausibility and, in my view, there are also some basic arguments about democracy that preclude it (see below). Others have tended to return to earlier traditions in socialism—utopianism, guild socialism, anarchism, localism—arguing that the problem was that one or other of these variants was pushed to the margins. The recovery of socialism, it is implied, depends upon these ideas now occupying center stage. I agree that such traditions contain valuable critiques of the dominant ones that could now contribute to the future of socialism, but doubt whether any of them individually contains the key to future success.

The Relevance of Socialist Ideas

How then might socialists respond appropriately in the current situation? One starting point would be to recognize that the difficulties are not primarily intellectual in nature. While there have always been some rich individuals who have been sympathetic to socialist ideas, it may be assumed that the doctrine will generally be resisted by privileged groups whose interests are threatened by it, and who will seek to undermine it through the power that they wield. The attempt to discredit the ideas of socialism is one aspect of this conflict, but the apparent success of this campaign probably owes more to the economic and political changes described in the previous section than to the ideological assault itself. Similarly, the prospects for its revival do not depend solely on its intellectual capacity, for it will face resistance from the forces benefiting from the status quo however strong its arguments are. Nevertheless, there is also a battle of ideas, and socialism needs to persuade ordinary people if it is to regain the initiative. A key element in its task of persuasion is to demonstrate that the basic aspects of the doctrine are still relevant.

The trend is currently toward a less regulated form of capitalism that is increasing inequalities both within and between states. The inequality within advanced capitalist societies, which had been marginally reduced in the middle period of the twentieth century, increased rapidly between the 1970s and the 1990s—particularly in the U.S. and the UK. Throughout the capitalist world, the life chances of the wealthy, in terms of health, life expectancy, educational opportunities, travel, and job satisfaction are vastly greater than those of the poor. However, intergenerational social mobility is very limited, partly because the barriers to downward movement from those born in the highest social classes mean that the positions at the top are already filled. For example, evidence in 2001 showed that in the UK 46% of the sons of men from the highest class origins remained in that social position, while only 6% fell to the lowest social class. At the other end of the scale, 38% of men from the lowest social class stayed there, with only 9% reaching the top social positions. Since there is some evidence that higher relative rates of social mobility are associated with lower income inequalities, it is also very significant that between 1979 and 1998–9 the inequality in real incomes rose sharply in the UK, with those in the bottom decile rising by 6% while those in the top 10% rose by 82%. Under the Labour Government, there was an improvement in

the relative position of the poorest, although overall inequality in society rose because of the sharp increase in the wealth of the top 1%. Such inequality is not fundamentally between individuals but is embedded in structures: the fact that some individuals, with particular talent or determination or luck, can rise from humble backgrounds does not affect the fact that the overwhelming majority cannot do so. Of course, the perception of the system as a meritocracy is functional to its legitimation, but this does not change its underlying basis. Similarly, the fact that poor people possess more than their grandparents had done in absolute terms helps sustain the belief that poverty and inequality are no longer fundamental problems in advanced capitalism; but poverty should be measured in relation to the wealth of contemporary society, rather than by historical standards.

Despite the relative wealth of many industrialized countries, poverty is omnipresent. This homeless family was photographed in New York City in 1996.

The structural inequality between the rich and poor countries of the world is clearly far greater than that within the capitalist core. Reliable comparative data over time are notoriously difficult to gather, but the UN's annual human development report in 2003 showed that fifty-four countries saw average income decline during the 1990s and twenty-one countries experienced an absolute decline in terms of human development (combining income, life expectancy, and literacy), compared with only four declining in this way in the previous decade. In this case, of course, the poverty that exists in much of the world is that of absolute destitution—the lack of food, drinking water, basic sanitation, healthcare, and education. Meanwhile, the richest 1% of the world's population now receive as much income as the poorest 57%, while the income of the twenty-five million richest Americans is the equivalent of that of almost two billion of the world's poorest people. This problem of global inequality might appear more urgent than that between the wealthy and the poor in the rich countries, but it is misleading to set one kind of inequality against another. A life of relative poverty in a rich country is damaging in all kinds of ways, and it is little consolation to know that the suffering of those in the poorest continents is much greater. Moreover, societies in which equality is valued are more likely to recognize the global dimensions of the problem than those in which it is not. It is no coincidence that Sweden has always made a far greater per capita contribution in aid and development to poor countries than the U.S.

Statistical data provide concrete evidence on measurable indicators of social and economic inequalities. However, socialists have never confined their case to these dimensions alone, but have also condemned inequality because it allocates the possibilities of human development so unevenly and arbitrarily. Behind the statistics are also the injustice of unequal power and unequal possibilities for intellectual and artistic creativity and personal fulfillment. Yet recognition of the enduring relevance of this aspect of the socialist critique of capitalism is clearly insufficient. In general, people know that poverty and inequality exist on a massive scale, but this does not make them socialists. The reasons for this are complex and may include the fact that many do not believe that capitalism is to blame. If so, one task for socialism in the twenty-first century is clearly to demonstrate the extent of capitalist responsibility for poverty and inequality and the reasons why the solutions that it can provide can only ever be partial. However, this immediately leads to questions of value.

Even if people were convinced that inequality was embedded in capitalism, this would not necessarily lead them toward socialist conclusions. In general, it is far easier to make the case against poverty than against inequality. Even the richest and most powerful corporate directors no doubt feel deeply uncomfortable when confronted with pictures of starving people and accept that this kind of poverty should not be allowed. However, they would be much less likely to accept equality as a value. Instead, they would argue that inequality is an inevitable part of the human condition—and that progress depends upon rewarding those with extra talent, energy, and ambition. Socialists would expect this of the very wealthy and powerful, but might hope that the majority of the population favored equality. Yet here too, socialism clearly faces an uphill struggle, for there is little sign that this value is currently widely shared, although there is certainly evidence of a far stronger belief in state intervention to provide support for those on low incomes in Europe than in the U.S.

Yet equality must surely remain a core value within socialism. Harold Laski (1893–1950) used to make the point very succinctly by saying that he had been born with a silver spoon in his mouth and advising people to

The British political scientist Harold Laski (1893–1950)—seen speaking before a subcommittee of the Senate Judiciary Committee in this April 6, 1938, photograph—traveled to the United States on several occasions. In his article "Why I Am a Marxist," he wrote of the U.S.: "I saw there, more nakedly than I had seen in Europe, the significance of the struggle between capital and labor. I learned how little meaning there can be in an abstract political liberty which is subdued to the control of an economic plutocracy."

be very careful in their choice of parents! This was his way of making the point that the distribution of life chances in accordance with the circumstances of birth could not be justified. Many would argue that such problems can be addressed by creating "equality of opportunity." However, as Zygmunt Bauman pointed out:

> "Equality of opportunity" means, in fact, equal chances to make the best of inequality; indeed, equality of opportunity is an empty notion unless the social setting to which it refers is structured on a basis of inequality. Thus the very use of the term, in a sense, sanctifies and accepts as a constant predicament what socialism is bent on annihilating.

Absolute equality between human beings will, of course, never be achieved. People are different in their talents, energies, interests, strength, and so on. In his *Critique of the Gotha Program* (1875), even Marx accepted that individuals were unequal, for "they would not be different individuals if they were not unequal." However, equality as a core value in socialism does not imply this unrealizable goal. Rather, it suggests the aspiration to create a society in which all have the possibility of fulfillment and in which life chances are not allocated by structural inequalities in social, economic, and political power. Of course, even this is a highly ambitious goal, but it can be used to evaluate and criticize societies and to push and prod them to become more equal. In relation to capitalism, this certainly involves calling for constant inroads into the privileges of ownership rather than assuming that "equality of opportunity" can be secured by active labor market policies and tinkering with the benefits systems. Similarly, on a world scale, socialists will continue to argue for trade and development policies that provide demonstrable benefits for poorer countries and groups.

Critics of socialism also condemn the commitment to equality by arguing that it will lead to the kind of drab uniformity associated with the former Soviet Union. But standardization is a choice rather than a necessity, and, as discussed in Chapter 1, was even celebrated as a utopia by one of the early socialists, Étienne Cabet. If such a version of equality could be conceived in advance, so too can a concept that rejects uniformity. In the twenty-first century, socialists should already have learned from new social movements that equality needs to celebrate diversity and difference.

The other socialist core values of cooperation and social solidarity also currently face difficulties in advanced capitalist countries. This is both because of the emphasis on individualism and competition in these societies, and because such notions as "social solidarity" can have negative connotations. Individual aspiration has been a central value within capitalism that has been internalized by populations, particularly as institutions promoting an alternative message have tended to decline. With a general ethos encouraging individualism, it becomes much more difficult for socialists to advocate cooperation and social solidarity. The terms perhaps now seem to suggest community living or perhaps a puritanical notion of social duty. Still worse, they might even imply the notion of forced cooperation, as in authoritarian regimes.

At the same time, it is also clear that many people in capitalist societies regret the absence of social solidarity or community. Many believe that there was once a greater sense of shared values and think that crime, drugs, violence, and the constant breakdown of relationships have something to do with the excessive individualism of contemporary life. Yet this can also be a theme of the political Right, which calls for the restoration of traditional values. At its worst, this can be coupled with racism and xenophobia, with the argument that social breakdown and the loss of the old sense of community have been caused by migrants or asylum seekers. In less extreme versions, the notion of community counterpoised to individualism often takes the form of nationalism.

All this has therefore become difficult terrain for socialists. They can certainly argue, with justification, that while some forms of socialism have always valued the commune or the living/working cooperative, this has never been true of all forms of socialism and need not be the model in the future. Again, socialists can also insist that the alleged antithesis between the individual and the community is a false one and that they have always believed that cooperation is as much a means to individual self-realization as a value for its own sake. Certainly, this has been combined with a strong commitment to the value of comradeship, which Marx expressed vividly in his *Economic and Philosophical Manuscripts* (1844) when talking of French workers:

> When the communist artisans unite, at first their purpose is propaganda, program etc. But at the same time, in uniting they acquire a new need, the need for society, and what appeared to be a means becomes an end. . . . Smoking, drinking, eating, etc. are no longer means of binding people together . . . The society, the organization, conversation, suffice in themselves, the brotherhood of man is no longer a phrase for them, but a truth, and the nobility of humankind shines out of faces hardened by toil.

This is perhaps a romantic view, but it encapsulates an important idea: that cooperation can lead to a sense of community and shared purpose to attain goals that cannot be realized through purely individual action. If this suggests voluntary cooperation, it must also be acknowledged that there may be elements of compulsion in the notion of social solidarity. For it assumes that part of the total wealth created by any society must be devoted to collective provision or public goods, such as health and education. Socialists will want this element to be as large as possible, but this will be contested on a variety of grounds that are at the heart of capitalist logic: for example, that those who are the most productive should keep the wealth because they have earned it, or that social redistribution undermines incentives to enterprise and rewards the idle. It also runs counter to the appeal to individual self-interest that has been cultivated by neoliberal ideology in recent years, promoting such attitudes as: "if I do not have children why should I have to pay for nurseries

Many socialists would argue that the interests of the community and the interests of the individual are one and the same. These principles led agricultural and industrial workers to unite in the formation of the Labor Party of the United States (later called the Farmer-Labor Party). Delegates to the party's first convention, held in Chicago in November of 1919, appear in this photograph.

out of taxation?" The notion of social solidarity remains far stronger in most European countries—and particularly in Scandinavia—than in the U.S., but it has been increasingly challenged in recent years.

Lessons and Prospects

If the critique of capitalism and the values of equality, cooperation, and social solidarity remain central to socialism, it is also necessary to look at it critically in the light of twentieth-century experience. What lessons should have been learned?

First, the socialism of the future must surely be democratic both in its own organizations and in the wider institutions in which it operates.

As already noted, the notion of equality in socialist thought has never been related simply to material resources, but has also referred to power relations. Both the positive contributions made by socialists to the democratization of advanced capitalist societies and the negative experiences of communist dictatorship have confirmed the anarchist argument that a political movement should prefigure the society that it seeks to create. Yet it is far easier to express such a commitment than to concretize it.

If socialists accept democracy, this involves acceptance of a multi-party system. One or more of these parties will be favored as a vehicle for promoting and implementing socialist policies for, despite all the obvious criticisms that can be made of them, parties remain indispensable agencies for change. However, this does not involve confining political activity to them or to established institutional channels. Social movements have demonstrated the effectiveness of single-issue campaigns, and various kinds of direct action have long-standing democratic legitimacy. Similarly, trade unions are clearly important means of defending and promoting the interests of working people, and the relative resilience of social democracy in Sweden has been related to the fact that trade union membership is particularly high there. All this suggests that a twenty-first-century socialist concept of democracy would seek to incorporate aspects of both the representative and more participatory traditions.

However, the democratic commitment can seem a little bland in cases where right-wing forces are prepared to use all forms of repression to defeat the Left. Nor, of course, does this refer only to local dictators, for many such regimes have been upheld by Western power. Sometimes even a commitment by revolutionaries to institute democracy can be used against them. For example, during the 1980s, the American government, which was arming the paramilitary forces in Nicaragua against the Sandinista regime, simultaneously coaxed that government into contesting elections to test its hold on power. However, the priority the Sandinistas then gave to the electoral strategy may have weakened the relationship with their peasant supporters, while the U.S. continued to destabilize the economy and support death squads. In these circumstances the Sandinistas lost the election in 1990. The argument that democracy should be an integral part of socialism needs to be set in an international context in which capitalist democracies have frequently failed to practice what they preach.

A second lesson from twentieth-century experience is that socialists still need to develop viable economic strategies. Chapter 2 showed that in both Cuba and Sweden social advances needed to be underpinned by economic success and these were threatened when the economy faltered. Clearly, there have been times when interventionist social policies have benefited economic performance, but in the last part of the twentieth century, the U.S. model of capitalism appeared to learn a lesson suggested by Keynes in 1925:

> If . . . capitalism is ultimately to defeat . . . Communism it is not enough that it should be economically more efficient—it must be many times as efficient.

Of course, socialists can respond that capitalism has failed because it has never eliminated its periodic crises of "boom" and "bust," and that it is wasteful and often corrupt. As the discussion on ecology in the previous chapter suggested, there are also many ways of evaluating economic success, and Keynes did not include sustainability in his definition of efficiency. However, in its own terms, it seemed that capitalism had achieved the objective that he had set it.

Some of the capitalist criticisms of centrally planned systems have been exaggerated, for they have had some successes both in economic development and in redistributing the wealth that has been created. The discussion of Cuba in Chapter 2 pointed to some dramatic improvements in healthcare, education, and rural-urban relationships through the planning mechanism. Nevertheless, at a certain stage of development, central planning has impeded innovation and introduced inefficiency and corruption; and it seems probable that the problems stem from the theoretical inadequacy of the conception itself. Many once believed that the Yugoslav system of self-management at regional level might offer a viable alternative to the centrally planned economy, but this too has now been severely criticized. Since the very rapid recent growth rates in China (and, to an extent, Vietnam) have been based on the controlled introduction of the capitalist market, there appears to be no really positive model of a socialist economy at present.

Because of the relative failure of centrally planned economies, the erosion of Keynesianism, and the apparent impracticability of taking privately owned international corporations into public control, from the 1980s onward many socialists began to consider alternative ways of combining plans and markets. The debate was initiated by Alec Nove in *The Economics of Feasible Socialism* in 1983 and attracted a great deal of interest, with many different versions—some of which veered more toward the plan and some more toward the market. This was also coupled with an interest in a variety of different forms of ownership, including cooperatives, decentralized public ownership, and mixed companies of both private and public capital. A further variation has been in schemes to use the state's purchasing power to provide support for ventures with growth and innovation potential. Some of these discussions have also incorporated the idea of sustainability so as to achieve the kinds of ecological goals discussed in Chapter 3. Many of these ideas have been very stimulating, but apart from the practical problems of winning support for such schemes, there are many remaining theoretical issues to be resolved. It seems that socialists have not yet been able, with any confidence, to put forward an alternative to the planned economy, on the one hand, or Keynesian demand management, on the other. Perhaps no single solution is possible or necessary, but given the centrality of the economy in the critique of capitalism, a range of viable socialist alternatives is surely needed.

A third lesson is that further thought needs to be devoted to the question of the level at which socialism is envisaged, for this is now more complex than ever. In general, the early socialists, the anarchists, and the

Greens sought to introduce their projects through decentralized communities, while Marxists, communists, and social democrats tended toward centralization at the level of the state (although there has been a move away from this in recent years). The problems in both approaches have been constant. Decentralization implies the possibilities of greater control, accountability, and sensitivity to local needs, but fails to explain how to secure any kind of equalization between areas with widely different existing resource levels, or how to handle highly conservative or reactionary local power systems. Centralization suggests a way of tackling the latter problems, but at the expense of local democracy.

The increasing internationalization of the economy in recent years has exacerbated these problems. If states (or, at least, most states) no longer wield sufficient power to bring about radical change, the traditional terms of the debate about level are anachronistic, and need to be recast in relation to the supranational, national, regional, and local. Nor is it even clear that this territorial approach is adequate, for power operates in different ways in different spheres, suggesting that functional divisions also need to be considered. Such debates have been particularly important within Europe and, during the 1980s and 1990s, many socialists believed that the EU might provide a framework in which a resolution of the problems would be possible. For example, there was support for the idea that Keynesian economic management could take place at EU level, while many other policies were decentralized. However, this does not seem very likely at present, with the current emphasis on tight monetary and anti-inflationary policies. Nor would a change in direction by the EU necessarily resolve the problems elsewhere. While some certainly believe that the EU could provide a model to the world that would differ very considerably from that of the U.S., others argue that the drivers to European

Some socialists believe that the existence of the European Union, which comprises twenty-seven sovereign states, does not necessarily promote the cause of socialism in its member nations. This 2006 photograph shows EU flags flying outside the Berlaymont building in Brussels, headquarters of the European Commission (the executive branch of the EU).

integration are inherently antisocialist. Questions about level also raise the more general questions of nationalism and internationalism.

As noted in Chapter 1, socialists have not always been internationalist in outlook. Some have regarded their own state so positively that they have effectively embraced nationalism, while others have concentrated on the construction of socialism at home without taking much interest in international developments. In many respects, the collapse of the Second International in 1914 is not simply an historical episode, but reflects a continuing phenomenon. For elements of residual patriotism are so deeply embedded that, when faced with an existential crisis, many socialists will rally to their own state.

Against this, I would argue that there are overwhelming reasons, both ethical and practical, for suggesting that twenty-first-century socialism must be internationalist. Yet it must be acknowledged that this position has also had its weaknesses, for many of its proponents have simplistically assumed nationalism would cease to be important and would be replaced by universal values. This was perhaps a form of Enlightenment thought that has been attacked by postmodernism and the proponents of identity politics. It is closely related to the issue of religion, which was also widely viewed by socialists as a premodern superstition that would be replaced by secularism. Many socialists would still argue that the current trends toward religious fundamentalism, and xenophobic forms of nationalism, are the result of pressures from capitalism and imperialism—precipitating anti-Western reactions. No doubt such arguments are partly valid, but twenty-first-century socialists will need to accept that particular identities (including those of nationality, ethnicity, and religion) have enduring importance to people, who often also possess multiple identities. Socialists will need to ensure that their doctrine is both compatible with this fact and perceived as being compatible.

Putting internationalism into practice is still more difficult. Opposition to imperialism in the shape of formal empires appears straightforward, but socialists have not always succeeded in converting an abstract internationalism into concrete policies. The global dimension may be the most important, but it is also the most complex, and it is unhelpful to pretend that there are simple solutions. All that can be said here is that the general direction of socialism should be to advance toward equality between countries at different levels of development and to attempt to construct forms of transnational solidarity and cooperation. While progress in these spheres would be difficult in any circumstances, the problems are currently vastly increased by the overweening power of the U.S. in the world. At present, Washington is opposed to any international regimes that might limit its autonomy and is willing to use its power to thwart their development. This situation is not likely to change in the near future, but there are important elements of opposition both from other states (including some of the most powerful) and global social movements which share the insistence of socialists that "another world is possible."

These remarks about the future of socialism have perhaps implied that it is a single doctrine, but the earlier chapters have constantly emphasized its varied traditions. What is their place in the future of socialism?

In general, there has been a tendency for each tradition to claim exclusive validity, but this book has been based on an underlying assumption that disputes such claims. Chapter 1 argued that each had contributed to the foundations of socialism; Chapter 2 concluded that both Swedish social democracy and Cuban communism had their successes and failures; and Chapter 3 suggested that feminism and ecology had simultaneously enriched and fragmented socialism. In my view, socialism should now be inclusive, even at the risk of eclecticism. For example, Marxists have often tended to put forward a framework purporting to provide both an overall theoretical explanation for the social sciences and a guide to action. However, I believe that there are strong arguments for disaggregating Marxist theory and combining elements of it with other traditions.

As a critique of capitalism, which explains its structures, dynamics, and propensity to crisis, Marx's work remains unsurpassed, and it also provides compelling insights into a whole range of social, political, and philosophical debates. However, there are areas in which his contribution is, in my view, minimal or unhelpful. For example, as Steven Lukes has argued, Marx's attempt to incorporate a theory of morality into his materialist interpretation of history is both unconvincing and provides no sufficient criteria for judging and, where necessary, condemning the actions of Marxist-inspired parties and regimes. Similarly, as demonstrated by both Joseph Femia and Norberto Bobbio, there is no adequate theory of democracy or rights in Marx's writings. This is perhaps not surprising since his purpose was to provide a critique of capitalism, and there was no universal suffrage at the time he was writing. Nevertheless, these must now be regarded as major omissions.

There is a still more fundamental problem with Marxism: its teleological dimension. In his preface to *A Contribution to the Critique of Political Economy*, quoted in the first chapter, Marx had insisted that "it is not the consciousness of men that determines their being but, on the contrary their social being that determines their consciousness." Generations of Marxists then interpreted this to mean that the proletariat would ultimately understand its objective position under capitalism and act as the universal class that would introduce socialism. Of course, all this left room for intense debates—particularly about the exact relationship between "objective" and "subjective" factors and between class and party. But in a very fundamental way, the issue of agency appeared to be resolved: capitalism would be overthrown and socialism established by the proletariat. In the early twenty-first century, with the fragmentation of the working classes, and the decline in their support for socialism, this no longer seems plausible. And if the proletariat will not necessarily take up its appointed task, who will? There is surely no clear answer to this question, nor any certainty that socialism will advance.

What can be maintained with confidence is that capitalism will not be able to resolve the problems and injustices that it causes, that there will be constant protests in one form or another, and that socialist arguments remain relevant. However, it is the task of socialists to help create that consciousness, not to assume, as Miliband once put it in a different context, that there is "an historical escalator . . . inevitably carrying them to the promised land."

Yet if Marx should not be treated with reverence as a prophet, it is equally inappropriate to ignore his work or to dismiss it, as many social democrats have done. Only purist Marxists and anti-Marxists will refuse to accept that the strongest elements of the theory can be combined with ethical and democratic ideas derived from other traditions.

Much of the contribution of these traditions has been implicit in the discussion above—for example, in the anarchist emphasis on current society prefiguring the future one, in the differing ideas of centralist and decentralist views about the level at which socialism should be constructed, and in debates about the relative merits of parties or direct action in transforming society. A synthesis between these different traditions may not be possible, and tensions will no doubt continue to exist within the socialist project. Thus, because of the concentration of power in states, parties, and leaders, the critical spirit that lay behind Proudhon's eloquence will continue to be necessary:

> To be governed is to be watched over, inspected, spied on, directed, legislated at, regulated, docketed, indoctrinated, preached at, controlled, assessed, weighed, censored, ordered about, by men who have neither the right nor the knowledge nor the virtue. . . . That's government, that's its justice, that's its morality!

However, change will also depend upon the use of public power and upon practical thinkers who concentrate on finding solutions to problems. This approach formed an important part of Swedish social democracy and underlay the attitude of the revisionist socialist Eduard Bernstein

(1850–1932) when he wrote: "To me that which is generally regarded as the ultimate aim of socialism is nothing, but the movement is everything." This is the mentality of incrementalists, who keep their feet planted firmly on the ground and are skeptical about grand projects of transformation. Yet surely socialism, rather than piecemeal reform, will have no future unless it also follows the advice of Oscar Wilde and remembers:

> A map of the world that does not include Utopia is not worth even glancing at, for it leaves out the one country at which Humanity is always landing. And when Humanity lands there, it looks out, and, seeing a better country, sets sail. Progress is the realization of Utopias.

A vision of a just and egalitarian society, in which all citizens enjoy equal opportunities—a vision that some would call utopian—underlies much of socialist thinking and activism. This illustration of Utopia was created for the title page of Thomas More's 1516 book of the same name. Note the ships surrounding the island, symbolic of its commercial prosperity.

REFERENCES

•

Chapter 1

Joll, James. *The Anarchists* (London: Eyre and Spottiswoode, 1964).

Knei-Paz, Baruch. *The Social and Political Thought of Leon Trotsky* (Oxford: Clarendon Press, 1979).

Lichtheim, George. *A Short History of Socialism* (London: Fontana, 1975).

Waters, Mary Alice. *Rosa Luxemburg Speaks* (New York: Pathfinder, 1994).

Chapter 2

Eckstein, Susan. *Back from the Future: Cuba under Castro* (Princeton: Princeton University Press, 1994).

Kapcia, Antoni. *Cuba—Island of Dreams* (Oxford: Berg, 2000).

Milner, Henry. *Sweden: Social Democracy in Practice* (Oxford: Oxford University Press, 1990).

Pérez-Stable, Marifeli. *The Cuban Revolution*, 2nd ed. (Oxford: Oxford University Press, 1999).

Pontusson, Jonas. "Sweden: After the Golden Age," in *Mapping the West European Left*, ed. Perry Anderson and Patrick Camiller (London: Verso, 1994).

Tilton, Tim. *The Political Theory of Swedish Social Democracy: Through Welfare State to Socialism* (Oxford: Clarendon Press, 1991).

Vanden, Henry E., and Gary Prevost. *Politics of Latin America: The Power Game* (Oxford: Oxford University Press, 2002).

Note: The recent statistics on comparative social expenditure are from Economic and Social Data Ranking by the European Institute of Japanese Studies on http:/web.hhs.se/personal/suzuki and *The Human Development Report: Cultural Liberty in Today's Diverse World* (New York: United Nations Development Program, 2004).

Chapter 3

Bahro, Rudolf. *Socialism and Survival* (London: Heretic Books, 1982).

Andrew Dobson. *Green Political Thought*, 3rd ed. (London: Routledge, 2000).

Eley, Geoff. *Forging Democracy: The History of the Left in Europe, 1850–2000* (Oxford: Oxford University Press, 2002).

Future Foundation. *Talking Equality* (London: Future Foundation, 2003).

Gruber, Helmut, and Pamela Graves (eds). *Women and Socialism—Socialism and Women: Europe Between the Two World Wars* (Oxford: Berghahn, 1999).

Lodziak, Conrad, and Jeremy Tatman. *André Gorz: A Critical Introduction* (London: Pluto Press, 1997).

Nicholson, Linda. "Feminism and Marx: Integrating Kinship with the Economic," in *Feminism as Critique*, ed. Seyla Benhabib and Drucilla Cornell (Oxford: Blackwell, 1987).

Rowbotham, Sheila. "The Women's Movement and Organizing for Socialism," in *Beyond the Fragments: Feminism and the Making of Socialism*, ed. Sheila Rowbotham, Lynne Segal, and Hilary Wainwright (London: Merlin Press, 1979).

Rowbotham, Sheila. "Dear Mr. Marx: A Letter from a Socialist Feminist," in *The Communist Manifesto Now*, Socialist Register 1998, ed. Leo Panitch and Colin Leys (London: Merlin Press, 1998).

Ryle, Martin. *Ecology and Socialism* (London: Radius, 1988).

Schechter, Darrow. *Radical Theories: Paths beyond Marxism and Social Democracy* (Manchester: Manchester University Press, 1994).

Soper, Kate. "Greening Prometheus: Marxism and Ecology," in *Socialism and the Limits of Liberalism*, ed. P. Osborne (London: Verso, 1991).

Soper, Kate. "Hedonist Revisionism," in *New Socialisms: Futures Beyond Globalization*, ed. Rob Albritton (London: Routledge, 2004).

Spretnak, Charlene, and Fritjof Capra. *Green Politics: The Global Promise* (London: Paladin, 1985).

Tong, Rosemary. *Feminist Thought: A Comprehensive Introduction* (London: Routledge, 1993).

Wainwright, Hilary. "Introduction," in *Beyond the Fragments: Feminism and the Making of Socialism*, ed. Sheila Rowbotham, Lynne Segal, and Hilary Wainwright (London: Merlin Press, 1979).

Weston, Joe. "The Greens, 'Nature,' and the Social Environment," in *Red and Green*, ed. Joe Weston (London: Pluto Press, 1986).

Chapter 4

Aber, Jens. "Some Causes of Social Security Expenditure Developments in Western Europe 1949–77," in *Social Policy and Social Welfare*, ed. M. Loney, D. Boswell, and J. Clarke (Milton Keynes: Open University Press, 1983).

Anderson, Perry. "Renewal," *New Left Review*, 1 (2000).

Bauman, Zygmunt. *Socialism: The Active Utopia* (London: Allen and Unwin, 1976).

BBC 2 Television, *A Century of Self*, Part 3 (April 2002).

Bobbio, Norberto. *Which Socialism?* (Minneapolis: University of Minnesota Press, 1987).

Breitenbach, Hans, Tom Burden, and David Coates. *Features of a Viable Socialism* (Hemel Hempstead: Harvester, 1990).

Carey, John. *The Faber Book of Utopias* (London: Faber, 1999).

Diamond, Patrick. "Rethinking Social Democracy—The Future of the Center-Left," in *Rethinking Social Democracy*, ed. Matt Browne and Patrick Diamond (London: Policy Network, 2003).

Eley, Geoff. *Forging Democracy: The History of the Left in Europe, 1850–2000* (Oxford: Oxford University Press, 2002).

Ellman, Michael. *Socialist Planning*, 2nd ed. (Cambridge: Cambridge University Press, 1989).

Femia, Joseph. *Marxism and Democracy* (Oxford: Clarendon Press, 1993).

Giddens, Anthony. *The Third Way: The Renewal of Social Democracy* (Cambridge: Polity Press, 1998).

Gorz, André. *Farewell to the Working Class: An Essay on Post-Industrial Socialism* (London: Pluto Press, 1982).

Gowan, Peter. *The Global Gamble: Washington's Faustian Bid for World Dominance* (London: Verso, 1999).

Harrington, Michael. *Socialism Past and Future* (London: Pluto Press, 1993).

Hobsbawm, Eric. *The Forward March of Labor Halted?* (London: Verso, 1981).

Hutton, Will. *The World We're In* (London: Little, Brown, 2002).

Jackson, Ben, and Paul Segal. *Why Inequality Matters* (London: Catalyst, 2004).

Joll, James. *The Anarchists* (London: Eyre and Spottiswoode, 1964).

Keegan, William. *The Specter of Capitalism: The Future of the World Economy after the Fall of Communism* (London: Vintage, 1993).

Lukes, Steven. *Marxism and Morality* (Oxford: Clarendon Press, 1985).

Miliband, Ralph. "The New Revisionism in Britain," *New Left Review*, 150 (1985).

Miliband, Ralph. "Reflections on the Crisis of the Communist Regimes," *New Left Review*, 177 (1989).

Mills, C. Wright. *The Marxists* (Harmondsworth: Penguin, 1975).

Performance and Innovation Unit. *Social Mobility: A Discussion Paper* (London: Prime Minister's Strategy Unit, 2001).

Pierson, Christopher. *Socialism after Communism: The New Market Socialism* (Cambridge: Polity Press, 1995).

Ravallion, Martin. "The Debate on Globalization, Poverty, and Inequality: Why Measurement Matters," *International Affairs*, vol. 79, no. 4 (2003).

Sassoon, Donald. *One Hundred Years of Socialism* (London: Taurus, 1996).

Schechter, Darrow. *Radical Theories: Paths beyond Marxism and Social Democracy* (Manchester: Manchester University Press, 1994).

Ussher, Kitty. "Is Rising Inequality a Problem? The UK Experience," in *Rethinking Social Democracy*, ed. Matt Browne and Patrick Diamond (London: Policy Network, 2003).

FURTHER READING

•

Any selection among the numerous works on the theory and practice of socialism is highly subjective, but the following offer a variety of approaches and viewpoints.

History

Shlomo Barer's monumental book *The Doctors of Revolution: Nineteenth-Century Thinkers Who Changed the World* (London: Thames and Hudson, 2000) provides a fascinating insight into both the ideas and personal histories of a whole range of socialist and anarchist thinkers. George Lichtheim, *A Short History of Socialism* (London: Fontana, 1975), remains a stimulating overview of theory and history. Two complementary books on the development of European socialism are both informative and stimulating: Donald Sassoon, *One Hundred Years of Socialism* (London: Taurus, 1996), provides a very full analysis of the evolution of political parties and their ideological and theoretical debates, while Geoff Eley, *Forging Democracy: The History of the Left in Europe, 1850–2000* (Oxford: Oxford University Press, 2002), pays particular attention to socialist political culture. Another stimulating theoretical history, which suggests that traditional socialism is being replaced by new social movements, is Carl Boggs, *The Socialist Tradition: From Crisis to Decline* (London: Routledge, 1995).

General Theory

R. N. Berki, *Socialism* (London: Dent, 1975), like this book, argues that socialism may be viewed as a collection of traditions, although he defines them somewhat differently. Anthony Wright, *Socialisms: Theories and Practices* (Oxford: Oxford University Press, 1987), is a highly original interpretive essay, designed to demonstrate the nature of disagreements between socialists. There is, however, an implicit anti-Marxist message in the book, for which there is an antidote in Ralph Miliband, *Socialism for a Skeptical Age* (Cambridge: Polity Press, 1994), an attempt to reaffirm a form of Marxism that takes account of the failings and crimes of communist practices and the positive aspects of liberalism. Michael Harrington's *Socialism: Past and Future* (London: Pluto Press, 1993) offers a different kind of socialist commitment, one that pays particular attention to some of the key economic issues.

Traditions

Barbara Goodwin and Keith Taylor's work, *The Politics of Utopia: A Study in Theory and Practice* (London: Hutchinson, 1982), although not exclusively about socialist utopians, provides an excellent analysis of their work. James Joll, *The Anarchists* (London: Eyre and Spottiswoode, 1964), is particularly useful in explaining anarchist ideas in an historical context. The relationships between the anarchists and Marx are explored in Paul Thomas, *Karl Marx and the Anarchists* (London: Routledge and Kegan Paul, 1985), while those between the utopians and various Marxists are highlighted in Vincent Geoghegan's *Utopianism and Marxism* (London: Methuen, 1987).

There is an immense literature on Marx and Marxism from a variety of ideological and theoretical perspectives. For this very reason, there are great advantages in reading some of the original material and there are excellent selections in Lewis Feuer (ed.), *Marx and Engels: Basic Writings* (London: Fontana, 1984), and David McLellan (ed.), *Karl Marx: Selected Writings* (Oxford: Oxford University Press, 2000). David McLellan has also written some of the clearest short interpretations of Marxism in *Marx: A Modern Master* (London: Fontana, 1986) and *Engels* (London: Fontana, 1977). Although Francis Wheen, *Karl Marx* (London: Fourth Estate, 2000), is primarily biographical rather than theoretical, it does provide some very useful insights into the historical genesis of Marx's ideas. James Joll, *The Second International 1889–1914* (London: Routledge and Kegan Paul, 1974), is an overview of the Second International, and the theoretical clashes within it emerge clearly from Dick Geary, *Karl Kautsky* (Manchester: Manchester University Press, 1987), Mary-Alice Waters, *Rosa Luxemburg Speaks* (New York: Pathfinder, 1994), and C. Wright Mills, *The Marxists* (Harmondsworth: Penguin, 1975), chapter 8.

Leninism, the Bolshevik Revolution, and the split between communism and social democracy are all highly contentious subjects on which there is a massive literature. Robert C. Tucker, *The Lenin Anthology* (New York: Norton, 1975), is a useful selection of Lenin's writings, and Albert S. Lindemann, *The "Red Years": European Socialism versus Bolshevism* (London: University of California Press, 1974), provides a vivid historical account of the tensions over the formation of the Communist International. Ralph Miliband, *Marxism and Politics* (London: Merlin Press, 2003), considers various debates in Marxist theory and practice that first became prominent in the era of the Russian Revolution. Peter Beilharz, *Labor's Utopias: Bolshevism, Fabianism, Social Democracy* (London:

Routledge, 1992), provides insights into the assumptions underlying some of the different traditions.

From the New Left to the Current Era

Lin Chun, *The British New Left* (Edinburgh: Edinburgh University Press, 1993), goes far beyond Britain in exploring the ideological ferment after the mid-1950s. Sheila Rowbotham, Lynne Segal, and Hilary Wainwright, *Beyond the Fragments: Feminism and the Making of Socialism* (London: Merlin Press, 1979), provides a contemporary insight into the ways in which feminism challenged conventional interpretations of socialism, and David Pepper, *Eco-Socialism: From Deep Ecology to Social Justice* (London: Routledge, 1993), explores the relationships between green thought and socialism. Norberto Bobbio, *Which Socialism?* (Minneapolis: University of Minnesota Press, 1987), attempts to define a new form of socialism building on liberalism, while Darrow Schechter, *Radical Theories: Paths beyond Marxism and Social Democracy* (Manchester: Manchester University Press, 1994), seeks to rediscover current relevance in submerged socialist traditions. Anthony Giddens's *The Third Way and Its Critics* (Cambridge: Polity Press, 2000) both explains his influential attempt to redefine social democracy and answers his critics, while Christopher Pierson, *Socialism after Communism: The New Market Socialism* (Cambridge: Polity Press, 1995), provides an excellent analysis of the causes and nature of the difficulties after the mid-1970s and subjects the notion of market socialism to critical scrutiny.

INDEX

•

Note: Page numbers in *italics* include illustrations and photographs/captions.

PICTURE CREDITS

•

76: LC-DIG-hec-25357; 110: LC-DIG-ggbain-25077; 172: LC-DIG-hec-24354; 176–77: LC-USZ62-63376

MARY EVANS PICTURE LIBRARY: ii, 17

SHUTTERSTOCK: 50: © Olga Utlyakova; 150: © Monkey Business Images

COURTESY OF WIKIMEDIA COMMONS: 7: Robert Owen statue - Manchester - April 11 2005.jpg/Author: Tagishsimon; 8–9: New Lanark buildings 2009.jpg/Author: mrpbps; 14: Potrait Pierre-Joseph Proudhon.jpg/User: Tailok; 18: Construction d'une barricade.jpg/Author: Loki11; 27: Lumea Noua St si Lit 1895.jpg/Author: Tantal/Source: *Magazin Istoric*/User: Dahn; 38: Lenin CL Colour.jpg/Author: Soyuzfoto/User: Militaryace; 60: Riksdagshuset (2625154069).jpg/Author: Benoît Derrier/Upload by Pieter Kuiper; 66–67: Storstrejk.jpg/Source: *Klass i rörelse: Arbetarrörelsen i svensk samhällsomvandling*, p. 39/User: Popperipopp; 73: Sweden euro3.jpg/Author: Dima1; 83: Che SClara.jpg/Source: Oficina de Asuntos Históricos de Cuba, Publicada en la Revista Verde Oliva 1959/User: Jan R; 127: View of Chernobyl taken from Pripyat.JPG/Author: Jason Minshull; 136: Bdk-oldenburg-2005-kuenast.jpg/Author: Till Westermayer; 147: George H. W. Bush and Margaret Thatcher at Chequers.jpg/Author: White House Photo Office/Source: http://www.margaretthatcher.org/multimedia/displaydocument.asp?docid=109631/User: Happyme22; 158: Tygodnik Solidarnosc 1981 lipiec.jpg/Author: Julo; 182: European flag outside the Commission.jpg/Author: Xavier Häpe; 187: Insel Utopia.png/Source: Rudi Palla, *Die Kunst Kinder zu kneten* (Frankfurt am Main: Eichborn Verlag, 1997), S. 35, ISBN 3-8218-4468-X/User: Lewenstein

BRIEF INSIGHTS

•

A series of concise, engrossing, and enlightening books that explore every subject under the sun with unique insight.

Available now or coming soon:

THE AMERICAN PRESIDENCY

ARCHITECTURE

ATHEISM

THE BIBLE

BUDDHISM

CHRISTIANITY

CLASSICAL MYTHOLOGY

CLASSICS

CONSCIOUSNESS

THE CRUSADES

ECONOMICS

EXISTENTIALISM

GALILEO

GANDHI

GLOBALIZATION

HISTORY

INTERNATIONAL RELATIONS

JUDAISM

KAFKA

LITERARY THEORY

LOGIC

MACHIAVELLI

MARX

MATHEMATICS

MODERN CHINA

MUSIC

NELSON MANDELA

PAUL

PHILOSOPHY

PLATO

POSTMODERNISM

RENAISSANCE ART

RUSSIAN LITERATURE

SEXUALITY

SHAKESPEARE

SOCIAL AND CULTURAL ANTHROPOLOGY

SOCIALISM

STATISTICS

THE TUDORS

THE VOID